THE
WORD
DISCLOSED

REVISED AND EXPANDED

THE
WORD
DISCLOSED

PREACHING
THE GOSPEL OF JOHN

GAIL R. O'DAY

CHALICE
PRESS

ST. LOUIS, MISSOURI

Cover art: © The Crosiers. Detail from stained-glass window,
        St. Augustine Church, Winnipeg, Manitoba, Canada
Cover design: Elizabeth Wright
Interior design: Hui-chu Wang
Art direction: Elizabeth Wright

This book is printed on acid-free, recycled paper.

Visit Chalice Press on the World Wide Web at
www.chalicepress.com

10 9 8 7 6 5 4 3 2 1   02 03 04 05 06 07

Library of Congress Cataloging–in–Publication Data
O'Day, Gail R., 1954-
    The Word disclosed : preaching the Gospel of John / Gail O'Day.
        p. cm.
    Includes bibliographical references and index.
    ISBN 0-8272-4245-X (alk. paper)
    1. Bible. N.T. John–Criticism, interpretation, etc. 2. Bible. N.T.
    John–Homiletical use. I. Title.
BS2615.52 .O33 2002
226.5'06—dc21

                                                      2002003062

In memory of William A. Beardslee

"And now faith, hope, and love abide, these three;
and the greatest of these is love."
1 Corinthians 13:13

Contents

Introduction

The aim of this book is to provide fresh access to the Fourth Gospel, for preacher and congregation alike, so that Johannine texts that frequently seem so elusive and frustrating may more fully become a part of the vital life of the church. The Johannine Jesus speaks powerfully to us, and if we can attune our ears to listen to the particular cadences of the Fourth Gospel, our preaching from that gospel will be empowered and empowering in new ways.

The task of preaching a Fourth Gospel text is often the true test for a preacher, because the Fourth Gospel texts are so different from what we have come to expect gospel texts to be like. Very few of our "beloved" Jesus stories are found in the Fourth Gospel, and rarely do we quote the words of the Johannine Jesus in our teachings. It is the Jesus narrated by Matthew, Mark, and Luke whom the church meets most regularly in story, song, and worship. Texts from the synoptic gospels, not John, are the mainstay of a preacher's repertoire. The three-year lectionary cycle reinforces the notion that John somehow does not fit in the regular rhythms of church life. Each of the synoptic gospels has an entire lectionary cycle devoted to readings from it, whereas readings from John are interspersed throughout the three cycles. Lessons from John occur most regularly at the highest liturgical seasons of the year, especially Lent and Easter, and while this is an important use of John, this pattern can suggest that John needs to be kept "special" and cannot or does not speak regularly to the shape of our lives.

1

Yet it is not only the synoptic portraits of Jesus that the early church passed on to later generations as authoritative for our lives and faith. The canon reflects the conviction of the earliest Christians that the Johannine portrait is as necessary a conversation partner as the other three gospels. The challenge to the preacher is to enter into conversation with John and to invite the worshiping congregation into that conversation as well.

The purpose of this book is twofold: to make the gospel of John available for the church's preaching in new ways, and at the same time to use the lens of the gospel of John to think more generally about the shape of preaching in the contemporary church. There is a tendency in the contemporary church situation to reduce biblical stories to a central point, a thesis, or one pivotal teaching. This manner of handling the biblical texts seems both to assume and suggest that once we arrive at this central kernel of the truth, we have correctly understood and appropriated the text. The paragraph and section titles that many translations of the Bible provide encourage this kind of reductionist reading of the text, because those titles seduce us into believing that they capture and communicate what the text is "about."

The preacher in particular falls prey to this tendency, as he or she attempts to make clear to the congregation in a limited period of time the message of the lessons for a given Sunday. The manner in which passages for sermon texts are selected, seen most clearly in the lectionary cycles that neatly parcel out scripture into "manageable" units, encourages the impulse to determine succinctly what the text is "about" and then preach as if one's task is to transfer that meaning to the congregation. With the more familiar lectionary selections, in particular the gospel readings, the task of determining what the text is "about" becomes increasingly laborious and unfruitful, because preacher and congregation both already think they know what the familiar stories say. When preachers approach the biblical texts with the discovery of the essential kernel predominantly in view, the possibilities that the biblical texts offer for proclamation are inevitably limited. The sermon too readily is reduced to anecdotal storytelling, the transmittal of moral platitudes, or worse, the preacher's thoughts for the day, without reflecting the intensity, challenge, and liveliness that characterize biblical literature.

The church needs to rethink the way we approach biblical texts and the way we understand the task of preaching. The narrative texts of the Bible are more than just story lines that can be summarized, condensed, and paraphrased. When one reduces a biblical narrative to a simple story line or a single moral or ethical emphasis, the speaker may still be telling a story, but he or she will no longer be proclaiming the biblical story. Such summary and paraphrasing of the biblical story preclude genuine engagement with the biblical text, because such summary and paraphrasing place us in the domain of abstractions, generalities, and propositions, and that is not the domain of the Bible and biblical faith.

When we approach a biblical narrative, we need to ask ourselves if what we think we know about the story and its message prevents us from coming into direct contact with the text and from engaging with the particularities of that text as the subject of proclamation. We need to ask ourselves if we move too quickly away from the text itself—from what the narrative does and how the story flows—to focus instead on some outline of the events, some central point, on what the text is "about." We need to take a closer look at the text itself, to linger with the text, to ask not only what the biblical story says but how it says it. The theater provides a helpful parallel in understanding this relationship between the what and how of the biblical text. When we go to the theater, we may already know the content of the play, but each performance allows the play to be heard anew.

The way that biblical stories are told, therefore, is neither gratuitous nor expendable. Preachers need to take the mode of biblical storytelling seriously, because the promise for the renewal and resurgence of biblical preaching rests in attentiveness to the particulars of that mode. For example, we readily recognize that the New Testament narratives, particularly the gospels, are composed of different literary forms and types of literary expression—miracle story, parable, pronouncement story, discourse, dialogue, proverb, and so on. When we read the gospels, we are not reading a sequence of propositions about Jesus, nor are we reading disembodied theological texts. Rather, we are reading stories in which narrative and theology are interdependent and inextricably intertwined. The way the gospels tell their stories of Jesus is inseparable from what is being said about Jesus. No gospel portrait of Jesus exists without its distinctive narrative vehicle. To separate the two, biblical narrative and theology, is to miss the essence of the biblical text and to do a disservice to biblical faith.

But how frequently do our sermons, both in preaching style and content, reflect this richness of biblical form and mode of expression? We know from our own everyday experience that how we say something is as important as what we say—"You know I love you" communicates one thing when spoken in anger, another when it begins a litany of complaints, and another when it is spoken in joyous laughter. Yet we often do not attend to the communications of the Bible as carefully as we do to one another's. Instead of listening to what and how scripture is speaking to us, allowing the biblical text to shape our sermons, we frequently allow our sermons to shape the text, narrowing the text to "usable" sermon material, to "what will preach" (an expression that echoes through the halls of every seminary).

When preachers allow the concerns and demands of the sermon to supersede the concerns and demands of the text, we practice proclamation in reverse. In order to proclaim the biblical texts faithfully, we must first allow ourselves to enter into the texts, to be shaped by the biblical stories in all their diversity and rough edges, and then move from that participation in the text to proclamation. Such proclamation will be able to capture and communicate not simply the subject matter of the story, the "point" of the story, but also the dynamics of the story, how it says what it says. If we attend to the ways in which the biblical texts themselves invite us to listen to them, and we try to replicate this invitation in our preaching, then congregations are not deprived of the experience of the text, but are transformed by their own engagement with the biblical material.

Careful reading of biblical texts, analysis attentive to the particularities of the way each text is composed, is therefore not something superimposed on, external to, or alien to theological and pastoral appropriation of biblical texts. Careful reading that takes the biblical texts most seriously always attends to the integration of storytelling and theology. To speak again in specific New Testament terms, when we read the gospels, we are reading texts in which the story of Jesus has been told in four different ways. The existence of four different gospels does not indicate that four different "points" about Jesus are being made, but that four different stories about Jesus are being told. We must be sensitive to and shaped by the way these four different stories are told. We cannot talk about the Jesus of the gospels without talking about these different ways of telling the story, but neither can we talk about the different storytelling modes of the gospels without talking about the Jesus they present. This twofold realization has important implications for how we preach. In a specific New Testament context, we want to ask how we encounter Jesus in the gospel texts and how we can most appropriately and faithfully communicate the Jesus of these texts.

In this book, I will focus on these general concerns about the relationship between the distinctive character of biblical texts and the subsequent character and shape of our sermons on the gospel of John. The book will approach John from two complementary perspectives: (1) How does the Johannine text lead us into its story of Jesus; and (2) How do we then lead and draw out what we discover in the text? The book provides studies of four major Johannine texts (Jn. 3, 4, 9, and 11), as well as sermons on other texts from John, as a way of inviting the preacher to reimagine what it could mean to live and preach out of these texts.

The four texts that are studied—Jesus and Nicodemus, Jesus and the Samaritan woman, Jesus and the healing of the man born blind, Jesus and the raising of Lazarus—belong to the

Lenten cycle for Year A in the Revised Common Lectionary. This is a place that they have long held in the history of the church, serving as Lenten preparatory texts for Easter baptism in the church's ancient liturgies.

One need only look at contemporary lectionary attempts to divide these texts into discrete units, however, to recognize that these Johannine texts present an immediate and direct challenge to conventional preaching practices. These four texts cannot be broken neatly into eight- to ten-verse units, because the Fourth Evangelist did not tell his stories that way. In the synoptic gospels, there are many short, compact stories that report events of Jesus' ministry, stories of healing, teaching, or exorcism. In the Fourth Gospel, however, as these four texts show, we almost never have similar compact story units with taut narration of events. Instead, we have long dialogues in which event and discourse are completely intertwined. No one aspect of the story stands in isolation, but all contribute to the story's narrative dynamic.

The church's preaching loses this dynamic, the intertwining of word and event, the involved interaction between Jesus and his dialogue partners, when preachers attempt to handle these Johannine stories as if they were the shorter stories of the synoptic gospels. When we move too rapidly to narrow these texts to what the stories are "about," we risk bypassing the way the stories move us along toward Jesus. Jumping too quickly away from the text itself to what we want to preach about the text, we manipulate the Johannine narrative and deprive ourselves and our congregations of the full experience of the Jesus whom John presents to us. The challenge to those of us who preach these texts is to allow ourselves and our hearers to move with John toward Jesus.

The four Johannine narratives that are explored in this book, then, provide a good starting point for thinking about preaching in new ways. Each of the chapters is written with a view toward preaching these Johannine texts at their given places in the liturgical calendar. But while the book is thus a kind of lectionary guide, that is not its primary intent. Rather, this book is an exposition of four Johannine texts in ways that provide fresh access to them for preaching.

In the analyses of John 3, 4, 9, and 11, I attempt to model for preachers the practice of careful reading mentioned above. In each of these studies, the starting point is the same: careful attention not only to what John says but to how John says it. Careful reading involves drawing on all the basic exegetical disciplines that are taught in seminary Bible classes—the passage's immediate and larger context in the gospel, its structure, issues of historical and social context, literary form, theological vocabulary, and the use of figurative language, to name a few. It draws on those disciplines with the recognition that those are the tools that make a careful reading possible, but they do not in and of themselves guarantee a careful reading. In order to apply the tools of exegesis in more than a mechanistic way, the preacher-interpreter must imagine himself or herself entering into a conversation with the Johannine text. The exegetical disciplines are the tools that make conversation possible—like a dictionary if one is trying to converse with someone who speaks a different language, or a road map for traveling through a foreign country—but simply using those tools is not the conversation. The conversation takes place when the interpreter creates a space for the biblical text to speak in its own voice. The more facility the interpreter gains in listening to that voice, the deeper the conversation will become, because then there really are two parties involved—the text and the interpreter.

Interpretation of John requires the discipline of careful reading because the Fourth Evangelist so thoroughly intertwines what he wants to say about Jesus with how he says it. The number of conversations and speeches in this gospel as well as the regular use of metaphor, symbol, and words with double meanings are all examples of the attention that the Fourth Evangelist gives to how the story is told. To distill any one Jesus story in the Fourth Gospel to its central "point" is not only a disservice to the gospel, but is essentially an interpretive strategy doomed to failure, because the Fourth Evangelist has told his story of Jesus in ways that intentionally resist reduction. For the Fourth Evangelist, the literary text is not the means to an end— the storytelling does not become expendable once one grasps the Fourth Evangelist's understanding of Jesus. Quite the opposite—the Fourth Evangelist's understanding of Jesus is not attainable for the interpreter apart from the story John tells about Jesus, because John's storytelling creates a world where gospel readers can come to experience Jesus for themselves. Reduce the story, and one reduces the experience of Jesus.

One of the interpretive emphases that emerges in each of the studies in this book is the literary strategies that the Fourth Evangelist employs to *show* and not simply *tell* the reader about God's presence in Jesus. In this way, the Fourth Evangelist draws the reader more readily into conversation not only with the story that is being told but with the Jesus that gives shape to this story. The task for the reader is to linger with this showing, to follow the gospel story through all its twists and turns and not to anticipate what the conclusion might be. If the interpreter begins to anticipate too much, then the conversation that characterizes careful reading is over, because the interpreter has begun to give the story its final shape, even if that shape differs from the one John gives the story.

The four textual studies are followed by sermons on John drawn from other parts of the lectionary. These sermons attempt to model another aspect of preaching practice—how the preacher, through his or her sermon, may enable the congregation to experience the good news of the gospel of John in its fullness. These sermons are shaped by the goal of creating a sermon world in which the pastoral and theological possibilities of the Fourth Gospel become real for the congregation. As preacher-interpreter, I try to allow what I have discovered in my careful reading of John to direct what and how I communicate with a congregation. In crafting the sermon, I try to find ways to open up the conversation that John and I have had to include the congregation as well. My starting point is not searching for contemporary relevance or "the preachable idea"; my starting point is the recognition that has come as a result of careful reading that John already proclaims a world of good news. My goal as a preacher is to find ways to invite the congregation into that world. When that world becomes their world, then it is possible to hear the good news.

If we are able to hear these texts in new ways, we may find that our preaching is genuinely transformed by the presence of God in Jesus that we encounter in this gospel. Perhaps, through such transformed preaching, we shall all receive "grace upon grace" (Jn. 1:16).

CHAPTER 1

John 3:1–17

Introduction

The reading for the second Sunday of Lent, Year A, in the Revised Common Lectionary (RCL) is John 3:1–17, the exchange between Jesus and Nicodemus. As has been discussed in the Introduction, the lengthy narratives of the Fourth Gospel do not accommodate themselves very easily to the demands of the lectionary, with the result that the Johannine narratives are often parceled in ways that work against the literary integrity of the unit. The lectionary's designation of John 3:1–17 as a discrete unit is an excellent example of this problem, because stopping the lesson at v. 17 interrupts a speech that continues through v. 21.

The relationship of 3:11–21 to 3:1–10 is notoriously difficult. The first difficulty is the shift from dialogue to what might best be termed a monologue. In John 3:1–10 Jesus and Nicodemus engage in conversation with each other: Nicodemus speaks in vv. 2, 4, and 9; Jesus speaks in vv. 3, 5–8, but as we will discuss below, the conversational character of the passage stops somewhat abruptly at v. 11. The second and knottier problem is the relationship of vv. 16–21 to what precedes. Commentary writers are divided as to whether these verses are spoken by Jesus in the context of the Nicodemus story, or whether they are the narrator's commentary on the Nicodemus story.[1] The NRSV and NIV both include vv. 16–21 in the speech of Jesus that begins at v. 11, which seems the best way to read these verses, and note the alternate reading in a footnote. Ending the lesson at v. 17 eliminates some of the ambiguity surrounding the speaker of vv. 18–21, but the RCL in effect creates a different conclusion to the Nicodemus story than the conclusion that the Fourth Evangelist created. It is therefore important that the preacher bear in mind the artificiality of the conclusion of this Lenten reading from John 3, and preach with an eye toward the whole passage. In particular it is important that whatever gospel claim the preacher hears in vv. 1–17 can be sustained in light of vv. 18–21 as well.

There is a similar, though not as extreme, truncated quality to the lectionary's designation of the beginning point of this lesson. The opening words of John 3:1 do have many of the marks of a story introduction, "Now there was a Pharisee," as they bring a new character into the scene. But these opening words are also vague, with no clear demarcation of either a new time or a new place. It seems likely that the scene into which Nicodemus enters is the same as that in the verses that immediately precede it, Jerusalem during the Passover festival (2:23–25).

Not only does John 2:23–25 provide the geographical and temporal context for the Nicodemus story, but also an important theological context:

> When he [Jesus] was in Jerusalem during the Passover festival, many believed in his name because they saw the signs that he was doing. But Jesus on his part would not

---

[1]See, for example, Raymond Brown, *The Gospel According to John (I–XII)*, vol. 29, *Anchor Bible* (Garden City, N.Y.: Doubleday, 1966), 147–49; and Rudolf Schnackenburg, *The Gospel According to St. John*, 3 vols. (New York: Seabury, 1982), 1:361. For a discussion of the reasons for reading verses 16–21 as the words of Jesus, see Gail R. O'Day, *The Gospel of John: Introduction, Commentary, and Reflections*, vol. 29, *New Interpreter's Bible* (Nashville: Abingdon Press, 1995), 548.

entrust himself to them, because he knew all people and needed no one to testify about anyone; for he himself knew what was in everyone.

These words establish a contrast between people's judgment and responses to Jesus and Jesus' judgment and responses to them. The many who believe in Jesus' name believe because they have seen Jesus perform signs, but Jesus does not entrust himself to such a response. The contrast between the two attitudes is brought out even more sharply in the Greek text, because the same verb, *pisteuo,* is used both for the people's acceptance of Jesus (v. 23) and Jesus' resistance to such response (v. 24). An English paraphrase that captures the repetition in the Greek might be, "Many believed in his name when they saw the signs that he did; but Jesus did not believe in them."

John 2:23–25 provides a disquieting background to the Nicodemus story. On its own, v. 23 is a positive development, in that many believe in Jesus' name. But v. 24 shows us something different, because this verse positions the reader to see, however briefly, with Jesus' eyes. Jesus knew that this profession of faith, however genuinely intended, was not to be trusted. How Jesus knew this is not supplied for the reader, and here the gap between Jesus' vision and knowledge and the reader's vision and knowledge is highlighted. Stories that come later in the gospel will confirm that faith that comes this easily and quickly, based on miraculous acts and not on the recognition of the presence of God to which those acts give access, will not endure. But for now these words reinforce the distance between what the reader knows and what Jesus knows, the distance between what we see and what is there to be seen.

John 2:23–25 also calls contemporary interpreters to reexamine both the goals and results of our engagement with biblical texts. Jesus' distrust in the face of the many people who believed in his name because of the signs they saw can serve as a warning when we are tempted to interpret Jesus too readily and to respond to Jesus too easily. When we read the stories of

Jesus for "signs," for single, simple points and names with which to categorize Jesus and his teachings, we respond in ways that resemble the response of those who saw Jesus at Passover. These verses suggest that faithful interpretation needs to be grounded on more than the ability to inventory what Jesus has done and, indeed, that even the most meticulous inventory may somehow be beside the point. To name what Jesus has done is not the same thing as understanding what Jesus has done. The challenge for contemporary interpreters, as it is for Nicodemus in the verses that follow, is to resist the inclination to define one's faith by readily perceptible signs, but to be open instead to the more demanding, and perhaps more inscrutable, presence of God in Jesus of which these signs give a glimpse.

The juxtaposition of John 2:23–25 and John 3:1–17 also provides an important example of the ways in which the mode of the text informs our experience of the text. In the summary report of 2:23–25, the Fourth Evangelist provides the reader with a distanced report of the interaction between Jesus and the crowd at Passover. The reader has only the Fourth Evangelist's summary account of what has transpired and of the quality and character of this transaction. As noted, these verses do not provide readers with their own experience of Jesus and this crowd who base their faith on signs. We are once removed from the crowd's experience of Jesus—and of Jesus' experience of the crowd—in this text, and the reader is primarily an observer of someone else's reported experience. The mode of narration of 2:23–25 does not invite the reader to participate in the text.

The reader's relationship to the text changes dramatically in the dialogue between Jesus and Nicodemus. In this text, the reader is given firsthand experience of one of the many who were impressed by the signs Jesus performed (cf. 2:23 and 3:2). The same themes raised by John 2:23–25—questions of belief, knowledge, and identity—are central to the dialogue with Nicodemus, but John 3:1–17 does not simply state these themes. Instead it embodies them. What is a report in 2:23–25 becomes a shared experience in 3:1–17, as the dialogue enables the reader to participate in questions of the nature of human response (cf. 2:23 and 3:2, 12), the contrast between human knowledge and Jesus' knowledge (cf. 2:25 and 3:2, 7, 9–11), and questions of human identity (2:25; 3:3–8) and Jesus' identity (3:13–15).

Given the complexities of the beginning and ending points of the lesson, its structure is deceptively simple:

I. Conversation between Jesus and Nicodemus (3:1–10)

II. Discourse by Jesus (3:11–17)

This outline shows that the focus in this story is on talking, and especially on what Jesus says and what Nicodemus hears. The dialogue between Jesus and Nicodemus does not provide the gospel reader with a ready-made set of conclusions. Nor does it explicitly enumerate themes and questions for the reader. Rather, questions are all evoked by the narration of Jesus' presence in the text. The richness of John 3:1–17 invites the reader to encounter Jesus at the same time Nicodemus does.

The Text

Conversation between Jesus and Nicodemus (3:1–10)

A plot summary of the Nicodemus story would resemble many stories in the synoptic gospels in which a Jewish religious authority comes to question Jesus: a Pharisee comes to Jesus; he states that he knows Jesus is a teacher who has come from God; he and Jesus engage in a conversation that ends in disagreement and misunderstanding. The bare bones of the Jesus and Nicodemus story recall Luke 10:25–37; 18:18–25; and 20, to name a few of the synoptic stories in which Jewish religious leaders come to Jesus with questions.

The simplicity and familiarity of this plot summary are deceptive, however. When one attends to the particulars of this meeting between Jesus and a Pharisee, one begins to sense that any plot summary only scratches the surface of this story. If the interpreter were to focus primarily on the fact of a night meeting between Jesus and a Pharisee or on one isolated teaching

(Jn. 3:3 or 3:16, for example), as if these elements communicate the "essence" of this story, he or she risks seeing and hearing less rather than more of the story that John so carefully tells here.

The rich storytelling dynamics of the Jesus and Nicodemus story make it a good beginning place to think through the tension in interpreting and preaching John that was discussed in the Introduction. The contemporary preacher's instinct, given the time constraints of a sermon, is often to find a meaningful and pithy digest of the biblical text that will succinctly and directly communicate the heart of the good news to the worshiping congregation. As we move through the Jesus and Nicodemus story, though, we will see that the Johannine Jesus' instinct is the exact opposite—the Jesus whom Nicodemus and gospel readers meet in this story is one whose words seem intentionally designed to confound even the possibility of pithy summaries.

As we engage John 3:1–17, then, we need to look at how John tells this story of Jesus and Nicodemus, how he moves the reader from character to character, from understanding to misunderstanding to the possibility of fresh understanding. The dynamics of this text are complex. If we pay careful attention to how this story unfolds, we may be rewarded with fresh insights into how we can unfold the good news in our preaching.

John 3:1–17 opens with two important introductory features: who Nicodemus is, and when he comes to Jesus. First, Nicodemus does not come to Jesus as a private citizen, as an anonymous anybody. Nicodemus is a man with impressive credentials: "There was a *Pharisee* named Nicodemus, a *leader of the Jews*" (3:1, italics added). Nicodemus's name is carefully encircled by the credentials that establish his status—his identity is defined by the public roles that he occupies. The literary structure of this verse, with its repetitive emphasis on Nicodemus's standing, makes it clear that Nicodemus does not come to Jesus as a man who stands on his own, but as a man who is surrounded by his community.

Second, Nicodemus comes to Jesus "by night" (v. 2). In a gospel that from its opening verses emphasizes the contrast between light and darkness (1:4–5), this reference to the time of Nicodemus's visit is more than an incidental detail. The visit under the cloak of darkness strikes a discordant note with the description of Nicodemus's status in 3:1. As a Pharisee and leader of the Jews, Nicodemus is a public figure, but he does not come to Jesus publicly. Nicodemus's night visit suggests that he wants to hide himself, and thus introduces a note of tension into the narrative.[2] That Nicodemus comes in darkness points to possible tension between Nicodemus and the community with whom his credentials so tightly link him, but also indicates possible tension between Nicodemus and Jesus.

In these introductory verses, the Fourth Evangelist simultaneously establishes and undercuts Nicodemus's identity. John 3:1 presents a powerful, authoritative public figure; 3:2a presents a man who comes to Jesus at night, thus rendering his public persona less visible and his self-assurance a facade. We are intentionally given mixed signals about who Nicodemus is and are not sure what to expect from this character.

Nicodemus's first words reinforce the opening image of Nicodemus as the public religious figure. Nicodemus, in his public identity, addresses Jesus with dignity and respect, from one teacher to another: "Rabbi, we know that you are a teacher who has come from God; for no one can do these signs that you do apart from the presence of God" (v. 2). Nicodemus speaks as a religious authority, drawing on his knowledge of God to support his views. The link between Nicodemus and his community, which appeared to be weakened by Nicodemus's night visit, is reestablished here, because Nicodemus does not

---

[2]Nicodemus is frequently understood by scholars who are interested in reconstructing the history of earliest Christianity as an example of a "crypto-Christian," Jewish Christians who are afraid to confess publicly their belief in Jesus. See M. de Jonge, "Nicodemus and Jesus," *Bulletin of the John Rylands University Library of Manchester* 53 (1971): 337–59. Raymond Brown, *The Community of the Beloved Disciple* (New York: Paulist Press, 1979), 71–73, gives a full discussion of crypto-Christians, but does not place Nicodemus in that group. See J. Louis Martyn, *History and Theology in the Fourth Gospel*, 2d ed. (Nashville: Abingdon Press, 1979) for a discussion of crypto-Christians and ways in which the tension between Jews and Christians may relate to the purpose of the Fourth Gospel.

speak just for himself. His use of the first person plural ("we know") implies that he speaks also for those whom he represents. The tension between Jesus and Nicodemus that the night visit suggests also seems to disappear, for Nicodemus's acknowledgment of Jesus as a teacher from God is an important affirmation of Jesus by a "ruler of the Jews."

Yet, in the context of John 2:23–25, the reader knows that the basis for Nicodemus's affirmation may be inadequate. Just like the people in Jerusalem to whom Jesus would not trust himself, Nicodemus's profession of Jesus as teacher from God is based on the evidence of signs. Will Jesus now trust himself to Nicodemus as he would not trust himself to the crowd (2:24)? Nicodemus's confident statement of who Jesus is ("we know") is diminished by the reasons he offers for his knowledge ("for no one can do these signs"). The Fourth Evangelist again simultaneously establishes and undercuts who Nicodemus is and what he says, with the result that the reader is left to wonder whether or not Jesus will accept Nicodemus's affirmation of him as a teacher from God.

Jesus' response to Nicodemus in v. 3 leaves the reader wondering still more, since Jesus neither directly affirms nor denies Nicodemus's statements, neither directly accepts nor rejects Nicodemus's affirmation of him. Jesus does not say to Nicodemus, "Yes, you are right, that is who I am," nor does he say, "No, you are incorrect, you do not know who I am." Instead Jesus responds with a teaching that returns the burden of interpretation and response to Nicodemus (and by extension, the reader). "If I am a teacher," Jesus implies, "then be taught by one of my teachings."

This first exchange between Jesus and Nicodemus illustrates well the difference in narrative style between simply *telling about* something (as in the summary report of 2:23–25) and *showing,* and points toward something to which we want to attend in preaching. In 2:23–25, as noted above, the reader is given only a passive role—to receive what he or she is *told* by the narrator. In 3:2–3, in contrast, the reader is given a much more active role because the narrator does not provide any assessment or conclusion about the conversation that is taking place. Instead, the narrator *shows* the reader all the twists and turns of the conversation. Jesus does not *tell* Nicodemus that he is a teacher, but rather proceeds to *show* Nicodemus that he is a teacher. Showing, rather than simply telling, enhances the reader's participation, because the reader is left to grapple with the meaning of what he or she is reading without the safety net of the narrator's summary remarks. Telling and showing in the gospel narrative set up very different experiences for the reader, and as we look toward preaching the Fourth Gospel, it is important to bear in mind the ways that we can recreate this range of experiences in our sermons.

The teaching with which Jesus responds to Nicodemus is: "Truly, truly, I say to you, unless one is born from above/ anew, one cannot see the kingdom of God" (3:3, author's translation). This is a well-known saying to all contemporary Christians. The expression "born again" is a part of Christian vocabulary quite apart from its original setting in the Jesus and Nicodemus story, as it has become the watchword for an entire strand of contemporary Christian experience.[3] Yet the level of familiarity with these words is not balanced by an equal level of understanding of what they actually mean and do in this story. The use of "born again" as a slogan assumes that we clearly and definitively understand the meaning of Jesus' saying, but, in actuality, the very words of this saying make a precise reading impossible. Conventional interpretations and applications of this verse ignore the critical fact that this saying is *intended* to be misunderstood.

The hinge of misunderstanding in John 3:3 is the Greek word *anothen,* which means both "from above" and "again."[4] This double meaning is lost in English translations, however, since

---

[3]See Eric W Gritsch, *Born Againism: Perspectives on a Movement* (Philadelphia: Fortress Press, 1982).

[4]The double meaning, "from above" and "again," is possible only in Greek. There is no Hebrew or Aramaic word with a similar double meaning.

there is no one English word that conveys the multiple meanings of the Greek word. In the NIV, for example, John 3:3 reads, "no one can see the kingdom of God unless he is born again," with "born from above" indicated in the footnotes as an alternate translation. The NRSV makes the opposite decision, translating 3:3 as "no one can see the kingdom of God without being born from above," with "born anew" indicated in the footnotes. Either translation inadequately captures the complex dynamics of this verse, because the translators have decided for the reader that one meaning is primary and the other secondary when the gospel text intends both meanings to be heard simultaneously. The reader is therefore denied the experience of deciphering and interpreting the double meaning that is inherent in the language of the text.

Translation from one language to another always alters meaning in some way, but this alteration becomes especially crucial when words with double or multiple meanings are involved. Both the NIV and the NRSV eliminate any ambiguity, which brings us back to the balance between showing and telling. The English translators' choices *tell* the contemporary reader what *anothen* means, whereas in his use of a word with an unavoidable double meaning, the Johannine Jesus *shows* Nicodemus, who has to decipher the complexity of the word on his own. Until we restore the intentional double meaning of *anothen* to this verse, we will be unable to interpret Jesus' words correctly. It is quite difficult to capture the double meaning of *anothen* in a crisp translation, so the teacher or preacher of this text must be intentional in how the verse is represented. If preference is given exclusively to one translation over another, then the richness of the text is diminished. Throughout this chapter I will either place both possible meanings side by side before the reader or listener (as in the translation above) or simply transliterate the Greek word, sacrificing crispness of translation in favor of coming closer to the experience of those who first heard this story.

The complexity of translating a word with a double meaning gives insight into Nicodemus's response to Jesus. Nicodemus understands only one meaning of Jesus' words, "born again," and is therefore unable to make any headway in his conversation with Jesus. Nicodemus can only focus quite concretely on the literal meaning of "born again," and therefore protests that what Jesus calls for is physiologically impossible: "How can anyone be born after having grown old? Can one enter a second time into the mother's womb and be born?" (v. 4). On the level at which Nicodemus understands Jesus, his questions are perfectly logical and appropriate. "I am an adult," says Nicodemus, "and you and I both know it is impossible for me to reenter my mother's womb, so don't talk to me about being born again." There is irony in Nicodemus's response, because his words are correct and incontestable on one level, but that level stands in conflict and tension with what Jesus intends by the expression to be "born *anothen*."

Even with this example of Nicodemus and his misunderstanding that derives from hearing only one meaning of *anothen*, we nonetheless are inclined to single-level interpretations of Jesus' words. Just as Nicodemus could only interpret "born again" on one level, contemporary appropriations of that expression also reduce its range of meaning. The irony of Nicodemus's response may be unwittingly operative in contemporary Christian response as well. Contemporary Christians may become so focused on a particular understanding of "born again" that there is no space to contemplate the fuller range of meanings implied by Jesus. As we will see below, the double meanings of "again" and "from above" are mutually enriching and mutually dependent.

Perhaps as further indication of the ways in which he truly is a teacher, Jesus' response to Nicodemus in vv. 5–8 does not call attention to what Nicodemus does not understand (the meaning of *anothen*), but instead attempts to move Nicodemus forward by working with what Nicodemus does grasp, however incompletely—the notion of birth. As noted, Nicodemus responds to Jesus' talk of birth *(gennao)* with his own birth language, not only repeating the verb *gennao,* but adding the image of the mother's womb. Nicodemus's reference to the mother's womb suggests that he does grasp that it is the birthing of a new being to which Jesus refers. Jesus amplifies this image of birthing in v. 5, because "being born of water" evokes the waters of the womb out of which new human beings emerge.

The new birth to which Jesus invites Nicodemus does not supplant the physical birth to which Nicodemus points, but adds to it: not born of water *or* Spirit, but water *and* Spirit. Jesus invites Nicodemus to enter the kingdom of God, in which the Spirit will play the same role as his flesh and blood mother: providing the womb of new birth. Nicodemus does not need to enter his mother's womb again, but he is called to enter the womb of the Spirit and to receive new life as a "child of God" (cf. Jn. 1:13). It is to this birth from the womb of the Spirit that Jesus points in v. 6, "What is born of the flesh is flesh, and what is born of the Spirit is spirit."

Contemporary certainty about the meaning of "born again" may impede full engagement with Jesus' invitation here. How often, for example, do church teachings about being born again focus on the birthing imagery of this expression? Vocabulary of birth and womb belong to the female partner in the birthing process in the ancient world, while begetting and generation belong to the male partner. The imagery here is unambiguously feminine. As Sandra Schneiders has put it so well, "Jesus was not speaking here of being 'engendered' by God, as of a male principle, but of being 'born' of God, as from a female principle."[5] The Spirit is portrayed as the womb of new life, yet this element of the expression is hardly visible in "born again" conversations. What we "know" can get in the way of what we are able to hear and receive.

---

[5]Sandra Schneiders, *Written that You May Believe: Encountering Jesus in the Fourth Gospel* (New York: Crossroad, 1999), 122.

The image of birth is not the only image with which Jesus attempts to teach Nicodemus the meaning of *anothen*. In v. 7, Jesus provides another interpretation of this expression through his use of the double image of spirit/wind *(pneuma)*. This second occurrence of a word with innate (and inevitable) double meaning reinforces that a simplistic interpretation does not and cannot apply in this dialogue. The image of the wind/spirit touches at the boundary of what is tangible and intangible, controllable and elusive. As it is with the wind/spirit, says Jesus, "so it is with every one who is born of the Spirit" (v. 8).

To what image of being born *anothen* does Jesus lead Nicodemus with the image of wind/spirit? Perhaps it is to an image of new birth and new life in which one's knowledge and confident assertions of how things are and how things can and must be are opened up to the unpredictable movements of the Spirit. The womb of the Spirit can birth a human being able to enter the kingdom of God, because the child of the Spirit is able (and willing) to envision new possibilities beyond the confines of established categories. We noted in the discussion of v. 2 how Nicodemus's identity is quite literally circumscribed by his formal credentials. The rigidity of this stands in marked contrast to the wind/spirit that blows where it wills (v. 8).

Again, Nicodemus and the reader are not simply *told* something, but are *shown* an image that they have to decipher in order to continue in the conversation with Jesus. The overlay of wind/spirit is a more familiar instance of double meaning, since it also occurs in Hebrew *(ruah),* and its imagery is present in the way the contemporary church talks about the movement and presence of the Spirit. Even when English translations pick one of its meanings to convey the sense of *pneuma,* we are still able to hear the resonances of the other meaning: the image of wind opens up the image of spirit to new levels of meaning that are possible only because of the double meaning. The ease with which we are able to hold wind/spirit together may provide a model for thinking about new ways to hold born again/from above together. Just as our sense of both wind and spirit is deepened by their overlap in the word *pneuma,* perhaps our sense of birth "again" and birth "from above" can be deepened by their overlap in the word *anothen.*

There is an important shift in personal pronouns in Jesus' words in v. 7 that the English translation masks. Jesus' opening words are addressed specifically to Nicodemus, "Do not be astonished (second person singular verb) that I said to you (second person singular pronoun)." But Jesus' concluding words address a more general audience, "it is necessary for you (second person plural pronoun) to be born *anothen.*" Nicodemus came to Jesus speaking for more than just himself (v. 2, "we know"). Jesus' response now also explicitly reaches beyond the two conversation partners to create a wider audience. The pronoun shift enables the reader to envision himself or herself included in the sweep of the second person plural pronoun, as part of the "you" to whom Jesus speaks of the necessity of birth *anothen.* Contemporary readers are invited to share with Nicodemus in envisioning the new birth of which Jesus speaks.

When Jesus finishes speaking, Nicodemus's immediate reaction is to ask Jesus, "How can these things be?" (v. 9). A literal translation of Nicodemus's question is, "How can these things be possible?" The images of birth anew/from above that Jesus has placed before Nicodemus—birth from the mother's womb and the Spirit's womb, birth shaped by the free movement of the wind/spirit—simply seem impossible to him. There are no easy answers here in what Jesus places before Nicodemus—as with the Spirit, nothing seems to stay fixed in one place—and Nicodemus has come to his conversational limit. He can only question Jesus in astonishment, reacting in the very way against which Jesus cautioned him. Nicodemus entered this conversation with Jesus as a bearer of knowledge, teacher to teacher (vv. 1–2), but he and his knowledge have been severely tested.

The reader can empathize with Nicodemus and his befuddlement. This Pharisee and the reader after him have been twisted and turned as together we move through the complexities of this dialogue.[6] And while we know that Nicodemus's response to Jesus is not the correct response, it is harder for us to know what the correct response would look like, or indeed, whether we are any more capable than Nicodemus of making it. Faithful preaching of the John 3 dialogue becomes increasingly challenging at this juncture, because the questioning and tension that this conversation generates in the reader must be maintained in any proclamation of this text. The preacher's goal here is not to supply his or her congregation with the "correct" response. To remove the tension would be to work against the very character of this passage, because it is in entering into the twists and turns with Nicodemus that the reader experiences Jesus. Rather, the preacher's goal here is to help congregation members discover how Nicodemus's conversation with Jesus may also be their conversation with Jesus.

Jesus' words in v. 10 ironically underscore the quality and extent of Nicodemus's knowledge. Jesus speaks to Nicodemus with a quick and penetrating irony that characterizes much of the dialogue of the Fourth Gospel, "Are you a teacher of Israel, and yet you do not understand these things?"[7] The quickness and bite of Jesus' words jolt the reader. We may momentarily feel a sense of superiority over Nicodemus, smugly thinking, "He really nailed you with that one, Nicodemus," until it slowly dawns on us that perhaps we have been nailed too. John 3 opened with Nicodemus's confidently asserting that "we *know* that you are a teacher come from God." But now Jesus turns that confident assertion back on Nicodemus and on the reader: "If you are a teacher, if you know, why don't you understand?" The issue of credentials, so deftly introduced in 3:1, is given an ironic twist

---

[6]For a now classic discussion of the social function of the narrative complexities in the Nicodemus story, see Wayne A. Meeks, "The Man from Heaven in Johannine Sectarianism," *Journal of Biblical Literature* 91 (1972): 44–72.

[7]For a discussion of irony in the Fourth Gospel, see Paul Duke, *Irony in the Fourth Gospel* (Atlanta: John Knox, 1985) and Gail R. O'Day, *Revelation in the Fourth Gospel: Narrative Mode and Theological Claim* (Philadelphia: Fortress, 1986).

by Jesus. The credentials and position may define the man, but they do not guarantee true knowledge and understanding.

Discourse by Jesus (3:11–17)

As noted earlier, at v. 11 the literary character of the John 3 passage changes. Whereas vv. 1–10 can legitimately be referred to as the story of Jesus and Nicodemus, that shorthand description does not hold after v. 11. Jesus' opening words in v. 11 seem specifically addressed to Nicodemus, since Jesus uses a second person singular pronoun. After those opening words, however, the focus of Jesus' words shifts, because all the remaining second person pronouns in vv. 11–12 are plural: "Very truly, I tell you (sing.), we speak of what we know and testify to what we have seen; yet *you* (pl.) do not receive our testimony. If I have told *you* (pl.) about earthly things and *you* do not believe (pl.) , how can *you* believe (pl.) if I tell *you* (pl.) about heavenly things?" From this point on, Nicodemus ceases to be a factor in the conversation; he never speaks again, and Jesus never again addresses him directly. Instead, the passage shifts from a dialogue between two characters to a monologue, spoken by Jesus to a much broader audience than Nicodemus. As at v. 7, this shift in personal pronouns brings the reader into the sweep of Jesus' words.

Unlike the earlier words of the dialogue, which have been an invitation to experience the kingdom of God, Jesus' words in vv. 11–12 sound more like a challenge and critique. Jesus' words state directly what the reader has sensed to this point in the dialogue—Nicodemus does not know, despite his claims to the contrary. And more decisively, Jesus' words assert that there has been ample opportunity for Nicodemus to know—"we speak," "we bear witness," "I have told you"—but Nicodemus has been unable to receive what has been offered. As a good teacher, Jesus began teaching Nicodemus the "easy" things, the earthly things, with the possibility of moving from there to the more complex teachings, the heavenly things. But as vv. 3–9 show, Nicodemus could not fathom even those teachings. He was never able to move beyond his own consternation at the single meaning of "born again" that he heard in Jesus' words. Nicodemus closed himself to the teaching of "heavenly things" when he could not comprehend the possibility of the birth *anothen* that Jesus lay before him.

Because of the shift in personal pronouns in vv. 11–12, readers are also implicated in the challenge of these verses. Jesus' words do not only question Nicodemus's ability to receive the heavenly things, but the plural "you" asks readers as well whether they are able to believe the possibilities of the kingdom of God that Jesus places before them. Jesus' words here recall his words to Nathanael in 1:47–51. Nathanael did believe the witness of an earthly thing, Jesus' recognition of him under the fig tree (1:48–49), and as a result was promised that he would also witness heavenly things, "the angels of God ascending and descending upon the Son of Man" (1:51). Nicodemus does not believe the earthly things, so Jesus questions whether he—and we—will be able to receive the heavenly things.

The continuation of Jesus' words in vv. 13–17, even after this challenge to Nicodemus and the reader, are an indication of the grace upon grace (1:16) that are at the heart of the revelation of God in Jesus and that define his character as a "teacher who has come from God." Even though Jesus has his doubts about his audience's ability to receive his testimony, he does not withhold that testimony, but instead gives the fullest statement of self-revelation to this point in the gospel story. The narrator has told the reader who Jesus is and Jesus' relationship to God in the Prologue (1:1–2), but vv. 13–17 are the first time in the gospel that Jesus himself confirms the truth of the words of the Prologue.

In these verses the reader is given insight into Jesus' identity and into what it means to speak of Jesus as a teacher from God. Nicodemus asserts that Jesus must be a teacher come from God, but v. 13 establishes the full meaning of that expression: "No one has ascended into heaven except the one who descended from heaven, the Son of Man." Jesus' words in v. 13 echo his words to Nathanael in 1:51, because they focus on the Son of Man as the place where the conversation between heaven and earth is located. Jesus can teach of the heavenly things because he has descended from heaven. It is not enough to say, as Nicodemus does, that God must be with Jesus in order for him to perform his signs. The more radical truth, which the ascent/descent formula highlights, is that Jesus is shaped by his intimate and ongoing relationship with God. Language of Jesus' descent is another way of speaking of the truth celebrated in 1:14: "The Word became flesh and lived among us."

If Jesus' relationship with God provides the framework for understanding the descent language, what provides the framework for understanding the language of Jesus' ascent? Verse 14 draws on the language of scripture to teach about the ascent: "And just as Moses lifted up the serpent in the wilderness, so must the Son of Man be lifted up" (cf. Num. 21:8–9). Just as the lifting of the serpent in the wilderness had life-giving power, so too does the "lifting up" of the Son of Man. John 3:14 is one of three statements about the "lifting up" of the Son of Man in John (see also 8:28; 12:32–34), all of which look forward to the lifting up of Jesus on the cross. These three sayings are similar to the three passion predictions in the synoptic gospels (Mk. 8:31; 9:31; 10:33–34; and par.).

For the third time in John 3:1–17 we have a word with a double meaning. "To lift up" translates the Greek verb *hupsoo*, but this Greek verb can also be translated as "exalt." (The Hebrew verb *nasa* has a similar double meaning; see Gen. 40:9–23.) As with *anothen* and *pneuma*, the overlay of two meanings in a single word is essential to what is being communicated. Because *hupsoo* simultaneously communicates physical lifting up, as well as exaltation, the Fourth Evangelist is able to use one word to communicate two simultaneous realities about the crucifixion. By saying that the crucifixion, the lifting up of Jesus on the cross, and the exaltation are one and the same, the Fourth Evangelist defines the life-giving power of Jesus' death. Jesus' exaltation is not delayed until the resurrection or the ascension; Jesus' exaltation begins with his gift of his life upon the cross. Understanding the double meaning of *hupsoo* makes the transition from v. 14 to v. 15 clear: eternal life is possible and available to the believer in the moment of lifting up, because when Jesus is lifted up, the fullness of the love of God in Jesus is made visible (cf. Jn. 10:14–16; 15:12–13).

Verses 13–15 also add an additional and final dimension to the expression "to be born *anothen*." Verses 3–8 focus on the question of human identity and on what is necessary for human participation in the kingdom of God. John 3:13–15 shows that this question of human identity must be informed by and can only be answered by who Jesus is. The Son of Man must be lifted up, so that "whoever believes in him may have eternal life" (v. 15). Or in other words, so that whoever believes in him can have and know life in another form, can be born *anothen*. To be born again and to be born from above really are two ways of speaking of the same reality, because to be born *again* is to be born *from above* in the lifting up of Jesus on the cross, in the exaltation of Jesus on the cross (cf. 13:31). Birth *anothen* is the new birth generated by the lifting up on the cross of the one who has descended from God, and this birth marks a genuine change in how life is defined. This change can neither be understood nor accomplished through human categories of spiritual and physical rebirth. It can only be accomplished in the cross. The point of origin for the one now born is with Jesus, not with ourselves.

The verses with which the lesson ends, vv. 16–17, abandon the language of metaphor (kingdom of God, birth) and words with double meanings *(anothen, pneuma, hupsoo)* to speak of this new possibility directly. These two verses name explicitly what is implicit in the figurative language of the rest of the passage— that the love of God for the world is what makes new life in Jesus possible.

The directness of the language of these verses is what places them, especially 3:16, among people's favorite Bible verses, verses that seem to sum up what it means to be Christian. There was a time when placards with simply the notation "John 3:16," minus the actual content of the verse, were visible everywhere, as if this shorthand somehow embodied the essence of Christian faith. The distillation of the Nicodemus story into this shorthand is highly ironic, because one of the main themes of John 3:1–17 is that the life of faith cannot be reduced to shorthand and to easily embraceable formulae. The words of John 3:16–17 are a catchy slogan apart from their context in the Nicodemus story, but they are empty of the experience of discovering new life with Jesus that the whole story offers.

Conclusion

The end of the Nicodemus story has an impact because of the reader's experience of and participation in the preceding narrative. The reader starts with Nicodemus's agreeing that Jesus is a teacher from God, but the dialogue shows the reader that Nicodemus really has no sense of what it means to speak of Jesus as the teacher from God. "Teacher from God" is the correct category, but Nicodemus's confident assertion supplies the wrong content. What he thinks a teacher from God is does not adequately convey who Jesus is. The categories with which Nicodemus approaches Jesus need to be reshaped and reconstituted by the direct encounter with Jesus. The Fourth Gospel allows the reader to participate in this reshaping and reconstitution by providing space in its narratives and dialogues for the reader to enter the text, and through the text the reader can encounter Jesus for himself or herself.

The contemporary church's attraction to John 3:16 notwithstanding, one cannot start the interpretation and proclamation of this passage at its end and come close to recreating the experience of Jesus contained for the reader in this passage. On the basis of the more direct statements of 3:11–17, one cannot interpret this text by saying, "What Jesus wanted Nicodemus to know is …" That is not how this text functions. To present this text simply as a vehicle through which one transmits data is to ignore the radical transformation of categories and the reorientation that has gone on in this conversation and for the reader. Yes, there is content, there is identifiable subject matter, but the transference of content is not the primary goal of this text. Such an understanding renders the biblical text itself expendable. The "lesson" of 3:1–17 is not to be found in a few catchy phrases, but lies in the transformative experience of Jesus that the text makes available.

When preaching John 3:1–17, therefore, we must be careful that we do not approach the text in the same way that Nicodemus approaches Jesus, certain that we know what this text is all about. If we approach the text in that way, our sermons will miss the richness of the dynamics of this text. We must allow our preaching to be shaped by the give-and-take between Jesus and Nicodemus, by the questions and answers, the understanding and misunderstanding. As we have moved through the text with Nicodemus in his struggle to understand Jesus and what he offers, we have found that we cannot assume automatically that we know (3:2) the correct answer to the question, "Who is Jesus?" We find instead that we need to allow the Fourth Evangelist to help us discover who and what Jesus is through the narrative dynamics of the text. It is the same with our preaching. We must allow our listeners to be shaped by the give-and-take between Jesus and Nicodemus. When we offer our listeners that experience, then they have the chance for their categories of the possible and impossible to be redefined and to experience for themselves the new life that Jesus offers.

CHAPTER 2

John 4:5–42

Introduction

The gospel lesson for the third Sunday of Lent, Year A, in the Revised Common Lectionary is John 4:5–42, Jesus in Samaria. In moving from John 3:1–17 to John 4:5–42, the lectionary moves the preacher and congregation from the religious and social center to the religious and social periphery. The individual with whom Jesus converses in John 4 is at the opposite end of the social, political, and religious spectrum from Nicodemus. Nicodemus is a male, a member of the Jewish religious establishment, a pillar of the Jewish community. The Samaritan woman is female, one of the despised Samaritans, with a complex personal history. The scene shifts from Jerusalem, the seat of religious orthodoxy, to Samaria, the seat of religious dissidence. The one constant in these two radically diverse settings is the presence of Jesus and his offer of himself and of new life. Jesus was not falsely impressed by Nicodemus's credentials and position, and Jesus will not be falsely condescending toward the Samaritan woman's lack of credentials and position. The question for the Samaritan woman, as it was for Nicodemus, is whether she will be willing to accept the gifts that Jesus offers.

By beginning the lesson at 4:5, the lectionary ignores the verses that explain how and why Jesus is in Samaria. After Jesus' meeting with Nicodemus, Jesus leaves Jerusalem and goes into the Judean countryside (3:22). Jesus then decides to leave Judea and head back to Galilee (4:3). After Jesus' decision to go to Galilee is recounted, the Fourth Evangelist adds another geographical notice, "But he had to go through Samaria" (4:4).

The opening verses of John 4 signal the importance of context in biblical interpretation and in preaching. In a limited sense, one sees the importance of context in what these verses contribute to the setting of the story that will unfold in vv. 5–42. When they are omitted, the lectionary preacher is missing the explanation for Jesus' presence in Samaria. But there is also a broader sense of context that these verses call to our attention. These verses provide a geographical and historical concreteness to the narrative that follows. Judea, Galilee, and Samaria are not simply place names, but are geographical realities that bring the map and terrain of the first century world into the twenty-first century. In order to understand what these verses say about Jesus' movements, it is crucial that the interpreter know how these regions relate to one another—that Galilee is north of Judea and that Samaria stands in the middle of the shortest route between the two. To bypass Samaria, one would have to go east across the Jordan and then return westward, adding time to the journey. It is also important that the interpreter understand something of the history of Samaritan/Jewish relations in the first century C.E., so that he or she can understand what it means for a pious Jew to travel through Samaria and can understand the many references to Jewish/Samaritan relations in the rest of the chapter.

The breach between Samaritans and Jews derived from the Assyrian occupation of northern Palestine in 721 B.C.E. (2 Kings 17), but this breach intensified about 200 B.C.E. in a dispute over the location of the cultic center. The Samaritans built a shrine on Mount Gerizim and claimed that this shrine, not the Jerusalem temple, was the center of cultic life. Jewish troops destroyed the shrine on Mount Gerizim in 128 B.C.E., and the rift between the two groups continued into Jesus' day. In addition, Jews and Samaritans disagreed over what constituted authoritative scripture, with the Samaritans accepting only the Pentateuch as authoritative. Many of the Samaritan woman's words, for example, 4:9, 12, 20, and 25 (see discussions below) require awareness of this background in order to be understood. John 4:5–42 is full of details that accurately reflect the texture of Jewish/Samaritan relationships, and this texture is intrinsic to recognizing the theological depth of the story.

The same care and attention to concrete detail that preachers give to the stories that they tell in their sermons should be given to the exegetical work that leads to the sermon. The concreteness of geography and history matters as much for our engagement with the first century world as they do for our engagement with our contemporary world. One of the responsibilities in preaching is to make the ancient world come alive for the contemporary congregation. This responsibility is not only enacted in the realm of theological truths and the experience of God, but also in the perhaps less glamorous realm of geography and history. The gospel of John proclaims that "The Word became flesh and lived among us" (1:14), and the particulars of where and how he lived make a difference. The more vividly we can imagine Jesus in his own world, the more vividly we can imagine him in ours.

The fact that Jesus "had to" go through Samaria, then, may simply reflect the geography of his day: the shortest route from Judea to Galilee was to pass through Samaria, though most Jewish travelers would pick an alternate route rather than come in contact with the Samaritans. Yet there may be another level of meaning to the necessity of this trip—the requirements of Jesus' vocation necessitated a trip through Samaria. Jesus' vocation compelled him to make the gift of God available to those whom Jewish religious orthodoxy deemed unworthy. His offer of the love and grace of God is not only for the well-connected, such as Nicodemus, but for those who live on the margins as well, such as the Samaritans. "Had to" *(dei)* may be used with a double meaning here, and this should not surprise the reader, since we have already seen how many times in the Nicodemus story the Fourth Evangelist used one word to say two things simultaneously. Whether there is more than geographical expediency here can only be judged by the outcome of the story, but it is important to notice that the possibility is signaled in these introductory verses. The two ways of understanding the necessity of the Samaritan sojourn are not unrelated to each other. Jesus may have been willing to accept the geographical necessity of the most direct route out of a conviction of the vocational necessity of his presence among the Samaritans. In 4:43, after he has spent two days with the Samaritans in their city, Jesus will resume his journey toward Galilee.

With this context in mind, it will be helpful to establish a structure for this long text. Afterward we will be able to proceed to a detailed analysis. John 4:5–42 consists of two blocks of dialogue: vv. 7–26, Jesus and the Samaritan woman, and vv. 31–38, Jesus and his disciples. Framing these two sections are sections of introduction (vv. 5–6), transition (vv. 27–30), and conclusion (vv. 39–42). The structure of this chapter can thus be outlined as follows:

   I. Introduction: Arrival at the Well (4:5–6)

   II. Conversation: Jesus and the Samaritan Woman (4:7–26)

   III. Transition: Return of the Disciples and Departure of the Woman (4:27–30)

   IV. Conversation: Jesus and the Disciples (4:31–38)

   V. Conclusion: Jesus and the Samaritan Townspeople (4:39–42)

This outline shows how much more complex this story is than the Nicodemus story. In the Nicodemus story, only two characters are involved, Jesus and Nicodemus, and the entire unit focuses on the conversation between the two characters. The only apparent movement of characters in the story is Nicodemus' disappearance at 3:11, and even this is not remarked upon or noted in the story. In John 4:4–42, however, the Fourth Evangelist has constructed a much more involved text. Three different sets of characters interact with Jesus—the Samaritan woman, the disciples, and the Samaritan townspeople. Not only are there more characters in this text, there is also considerable movement by these characters. The story narrates the arrival and departure of each set of characters from the well where Jesus is located (see 4:7, 8, 27, 28, 30, 40).

In the variety of characters who populate John 4:5–42 and the bustle of movement to and from the well, only one character remains constant—Jesus. Once Jesus arrives at the well in v. 6, he does not move from there until v. 40, when he goes to stay with the Samaritans in their city. John 4:5–42 is a carefully and elaborately constructed text, composed with narrative and literary intentionality. The stability of Jesus, highlighted by the continual movement of the other characters, is a mark of that intentionality. One clue for successfully navigating the many twists of this story is to keep our attention fixed on Jesus as we read and listen to this text. This may also provide a clue for preaching this text, since one interpretive task of the preacher of John 4 is to help the congregation fix its attention on Jesus.

As with the Nicodemus story, John 4:5–42 is more than the details of its story line. One could follow the headings of the outline given above and arrive at the following plot summary of John 5:4–42: Jesus has a conversation with a Samaritan woman and then has a conversation with his disciples. As a result of those two conversations, Jesus visits the Samaritan village, and Samaritans believe in him. But this plot summary does not come close to capturing either the character or the complexity of this text. As was the case with the Nicodemus story, reading John 4:5–42 requires more than simply reading for plot, themes, and theological "truths" that then can be abstracted in a sermon idea. Reading John 4:5–42 requires that the reader allow himself or herself to move into all dimensions of the conversations that are played out in the text, experiencing along with the Samaritan woman, the disciples, and the Samaritan villagers the range of responses to Jesus—from confusion to discovery to affirmation of faith. The Fourth Evangelist has provided us with a text that invites the reader to enter into its world and to participate in the transformation of categories and experience wrought by engagement with Jesus.

The Text
Introduction: Arrival at the Well (4:5–6)

John 4:5–6 provides a very detailed description of the setting for Jesus' conversation with the Samaritan woman. The city in Samaria where Jesus finds himself, Sychar, is described in terms that immediately bring the Old Testament to mind: "near the plot of ground that Jacob had given to his son Joseph. Jacob's well was there." Jesus has arrived at a place whose very location is defined by its relation to the patriarchal story.[1] This is important, since Jews and Samaritans were in agreement about the authority of the patriarchs for religious life. The traditions that are introduced in these opening verses will take on more importance as the story of John 4:5–42 unfolds.

Jesus arrives at Jacob's well in the middle of the day and sits down beside the well, wearied from his journey (v. 6). The detail about Jesus' fatigue adds a touch of realism to the story, but it also provides a transition to the next section. Jesus' fatigue from the journey provides the rationale for his request for a drink of water in v. 7.

---

[1] The Fourth Evangelist appears to be drawing on the Jacob traditions in Gen. 33:19; 48:22, and Josh. 24:32 in these verses. See Jerome H. Neyrey, "Jacob Traditions and the Interpretation of John 4:10–26," *Catholic Biblical Quarterly* 41 (1979): 419–37, and "The Jacob Allusions in John 1:51," *Catholic Biblical Quarterly* 44 (1982): 586–605.

These opening verses introduce several details that the rest of the text will develop. First, as mentioned earlier, they introduce the necessity of Jesus' presence in Samaria. As the reader moves through John 4:5–42, it will be important to consider whether Jesus is in Samaria because of a conviction about his vocation. Second, the person of Jacob figures prominently in these opening verses. The ground for a comparison between Jesus and Jacob is set. Third, Jesus' posture at the well is one of vulnerability and need. He is tired and sits to rest. In v. 7 Jesus makes his need known to the Samaritan woman.

Conversation: Jesus and the Samaritan Woman (4:7–26)

Verses 7–15

A Samaritan woman arrives at the well to draw water (v. 7), and the two central characters are now in place. Jesus begins the conversation with the woman with a request, expressed in the imperative: "Give me a drink" (v. 7). It is, on the surface, a simple enough request. Jesus is weary from his journey, and it is the middle of the day (v. 6). He is alone and without refreshment because his disciples have gone into the city to buy food (v. 8). Like Elijah requesting food and drink from the widow of Sidon (1 Kings 17:10–11), Jesus interrupts a woman in the midst of her household work to request a gesture of hospitality. Unlike the widow of Sidon, however, who shared with Elijah from the little that she had, the Samaritan woman does not respond to Jesus' request with an offer of water. Instead she greets his request with stunned amazement and consternation: "How is it that you, a Jew, ask a drink of me, a woman of Samaria?" (v. 9a).

From the Samaritan woman's perspective, Jesus has violated two societal conventions in requesting water from her. First, as the narrator's comment in verse 9c makes explicit, Jews did not invite contact with Samaritans, since Samaritans were understood to be ritually unclean. Jesus, however, by accepting the necessity of traveling through Samaria, has already demonstrated his willingness "to share things in common with Samaritans." In requesting water from the Samaritan woman, Jesus shows himself to be independent of traditional Jewish customs and expectations, but the Samaritan woman cannot see that.

Second, the Samaritan woman understands Jesus to be violating another deep-seated convention, that of male/female interaction. The woman's amazement that Jesus, a Jewish man, is speaking with her, a Samaritan woman, is echoed in the disciples' reaction when they arrive at the well in v. 27. A Jewish man did not initiate conversation with an unknown woman, and a teacher did not engage in public conversation with a woman.[2] There was no "good" reason for Jesus to be in conversation with this woman. By speaking with her, he violated both Jewish and Samaritan expectations.

The Samaritan woman is so taken aback by Jesus' violation of tradition that his need of hospitality is forgotten. She does not offer water to the tired traveler. She is unable to respond to Jesus, because his request violates the conventions and traditions around which she structures her life. She cannot move beyond Jesus' Jewishness and his maleness to respond to his need. She can only ask "how" in protest of the seeming impossibility of the situation, much as Nicodemus could only ask, "How can these things be?" in 3:9 (cf. 3:4 also).

Yet even though the Samaritan woman at this point is not able to respond to Jesus' request, her words do suggest that she is capable of seeing deeper meaning than what appears on the surface. She has turned a simple request for water into a question of identity and an issue of social contrasts—Jewish identity versus Samaritan identity, male identity versus female identity. Jesus will follow the woman's lead and continue the theme of identity in his response. He does not repeat his request for a drink,

---

[2]See Sandra Schneiders's discussion of the feminist implications of this conversation in *Written That You May Believe: Encountering Jesus in the Fourth Gospel* (New York: Crossroad, 1999), 126–48.

but instead probes more deeply into the identity of the one who is so bold as to request water from the woman: "If you knew the gift of God, and who it is that is saying to you, 'Give me a drink,' you would have asked him, and he would have given you living water" (v. 10).

In asking the Samaritan woman to recognize his identity, Jesus is asking one of the central questions in the Fourth Gospel. We have already seen this question in the Nicodemus story. Nicodemus thinks the answer to the "who is Jesus?" question is "a teacher from God," but John 3:1–17 shows that this answer is incomplete. The question of Jesus' identity will also be central in the texts of John 9 and 11, to which we will turn later. Here in 4:10 Jesus himself explicitly raises this question. By placing the question in Jesus' own mouth, the Fourth Evangelist signals its pivotal importance to the gospel story that is unfolding.

Jesus' words in v. 10, much like his words to Nicodemus in 3:5, move the conversation to a new level. Jesus greeted Nicodemus's acknowledgement that Jesus was a teacher from God with a teaching about new birth that moved the conversation beyond Nicodemus's expectations. In this text, Jesus moves the woman's words from a concern about Jewish and Samaritan identity to a concern with the identity of the gift of God and the one who is the source of living water. He offers an invitation to the woman: if she can identify the gift of God and the identity of the one with whom she speaks, then a dramatic role reversal will occur. Instead of being the one from whom water is requested, she will become the one to whom water is given.

More than the woman's role is transformed, however. The water that is available to be given is transformed too. Jesus requested well water from the woman; he offers her "living water" *(hydor zon)*. "Living water" can be understood in two ways. First, the expression can be understood as a description of a particular type of water: fresh, running water that comes from a spring, in contrast to water that is collected in cisterns and wells. But the expression also can have a metaphorical dimension:

"living" water is water that is brimming with life. Once again we find the Fourth Evangelist intentionally using words with a double meaning (cf. *anothen*, *pneuma*, *hupsoo* in John 3), intentionally using the richness of language to push beyond conventional assumptions and expectations. As in the occurrences of words with a double meaning in John 3, the ambiguity of the multiple levels of meaning is not immediately resolved— for the gospel character or for the reader. The combination of "living water" with the "gift of God" in v. 10 suggests that Jesus has more than spring water in mind here, but the text leaves all possibilities open.

This aspect of the language and literary style of the Fourth Gospel presents the same range of challenges and possibilities to the preacher as it does for the Samaritan woman and the gospel reader. There is no quick fix, no immediately available answer. Jesus does not announce in v. 10, "I am the gift of God," but instead offers, "*if you knew* the gift of God." The Samaritan woman has to listen to Jesus and make some decisions for herself about Jesus' words and the identity of the person with whom she is engaged in conversation. The preacher is challenged to resist the rush to an announcement that Jesus himself does not make here and instead follow the lead of Jesus, suggesting possibilities that engage the congregation in its own encounter with Jesus.

The Samaritan woman's response in vv. 11–12 illustrates the risks inherent in offering possibilities instead of clear answers. One cannot dictate the listener's response, and in this instance, it appears that the Samaritan woman has not understood the possibilities offered her by Jesus. He has offered her a new role, the one who receives, and a new gift, living water, but the woman acts as if she has heard none of that. All she seems to hear is that this Jewish man who moments ago was requesting water for himself because he had no way to get any from the well (v. 11), is now foolish enough to offer her living water. The woman does not recognize the ambiguity of the expression "living water" and reacts solely on the level of drinking water.

Just as Nicodemus heard only one level of the expression "to be born *anothen*" and therefore responded to Jesus' offer with protests of logical and physiological impossibility, so too the woman responds with protests of logical and material impossibility. "Sir, you have no bucket, and the well is deep. Where do you get that living water?" (v. 11). Jesus and the woman are conducting their conversation on two quite distinct levels.

In asking this "where" question, the Samaritan woman has asked a question that is plausible for both meanings of "living water." She wonders how it could be possible for this man, who just moments before had asked her for water, now to profess to be able to provide water for her, and not simply well water, but "living water," water from a spring. But the woman is only aware of the question's appropriateness in regard to the source of drinking water. She does not know that she has also asked a question that could enable her to answer the question Jesus asked her in v. 10. If she knew where Jesus gets the living water of which he speaks, she would also know who Jesus is. The reader of the Fourth Gospel knows the source and origin of Jesus and his gifts— they are from God (e.g., 3:35; 5:36; 7:29). Jesus himself is the ultimate gift of God, the one whom God gave for the world (3:16). The woman does not know this, however. She knows only that a Jew has violated convention by requesting water from her and is now making her an implausible offer of living spring water.

Verse 12 indicates that the woman thinks Jesus has done more than violate social conventions and logical expectations. His preposterous offer of water when he has nothing with which to draw is an affront to the traditions of Jacob. "Our father Jacob" was able to produce water from the well at Haran only by a miracle.[3] How could this strange Jew stand beside this well and

---

[3]The tradition that Jacob miraculously produced water from a well is not present in the Old Testament, but developed in later rabbinic literature. See Jose Ramon Diaz, "Palestinian Targum and the New Testament," *Novum Testamentum* 6 (1963): 76–77, and the Neyrey articles cited in note 1.

think he could produce living spring water? Is he "greater than our ancestor Jacob"?

This question is a universally recognized instance of Johannine irony.[4] The source of its irony is easy to spot: for the Fourth Evangelist and his readers, Jesus was indeed greater than Jacob. The irony of the woman's question is especially clear in the Greek. While one could read the English translation as if the woman were asking a genuine question to which she did not know the answer ("Are you greater than our ancestor Jacob?"), the Greek syntax makes clear that she does know the answer to her question and that the answer is a resounding No. The comparison between Jesus and Jacob, which was anticipated by the detailed description of the setting in vv. 5–6, is now made explicit. Again the woman's inability to penetrate Jesus' full identity comes to the surface. She is so confident of her assessment of the situation, of who Jesus is, of how he stands in relation to Jacob, that she cannot see and hear what is offered her. Jacob gave "us" the well; he drank from it; his cattle drank from it. His whole household was refreshed by Jacob's gift of water. How could this tired, thirsty Jew possibly offer any water that could surpass the water offered by Jacob?

Just as he did in his words in v. 10, Jesus follows the woman's lead here. If she wants to talk about the water that Jacob produced from this well, then he will too—but with a twist. He does not directly address the question of who is greater—he or Jacob. Instead, Jesus places his gift of water (vv. 13–14) next to Jacob's gift of water (v. 12), and invites the woman to choose. Will she choose the old water, which is abundant but does not quench thirst ("everyone who drinks of this water will be thirsty

---

[4]See Raymond Brown, *The Gospel According to John (I–XII)*, vol. 29, *Anchor Bible* (Garden City, N.Y.: Doubleday, 1966), 170; C. K. Barrett, *The Gospel According to St. John*, 2d ed. (Philadelphia, Westminster, 1974), 234. For a more detailed discussion of the irony of this verse, see Paul Duke, *Irony in the Fourth Gospel* (Atlanta: John Knox, 1985), 70, 94; R. Alan Culpepper, *Anatomy of the Fourth Gospel* (Philadelphia: Fortress Press, 1983), 172–76; and Gail R. O'Day, *Revelation in the Fourth Gospel: Narrative Mode and Theological Claim* (Philadelphia: Fortress, 1986), chapter 3. The irony of this verse is repeated in 8:53, when the Jews ask, "Are you greater than our father Abraham?"

again," v. 13), or will she choose the new water, which quenches thirst and becomes in those who drink "a spring of water gushing up to eternal life" (v. 14)? Jesus makes a play on both meanings of "living water" in v. 14, because the metaphorical water that is the source of life is described as a running spring.

In John 3, Nicodemus was offered the promise of new life, of being born *anothen*. Now the Samaritan woman is also offered the promise of new life, but the promise comes through the imagery of water rather than that of birth. Yet this imagery is not completely distinct from the language that Jesus used with Nicodemus, since Jesus spoke to Nicodemus of birth of "*water and spirit*" (Jn. 3:5). In John 7:37–39, Jesus refers to the Spirit with the same imagery of living water that is used at 4:14 (*hydor zon,* used in the genitive case at 7:38). When all three passages are placed in conversation with one another, the relationship between the invitation that Jesus makes to Nicodemus and that which he makes to the Samaritan woman becomes clear. Jesus offers the unending presence of God: like the spirit/wind that blows where it wills, like streams of gushing water that never run dry. The promise of eternal life that Jesus makes to Nicodemus in 3:15 and the Samaritan woman in 4:14 is another way of talking about the unending presence of God.

Is Jesus greater than "our father Jacob"? Neither Jesus nor the Fourth Evangelist answers that question explicitly. The Samaritan woman and the reader must ponder what Jesus offers and decide that question for themselves. In preaching this text, the preacher must allow the congregation to arrive at the same moment of decision, to sense for themselves what Jesus is offering and what is at stake in rejecting or accepting the offer. Jesus cannot make the decision for the Samaritan woman. He can only offer her living water and invite her to a transformed life. Similarly, the preacher cannot preempt the decision-making process for those to whom he or she preaches. The preacher can only offer the congregation living water and invite them to a transformed life. It is through the sermon that the offer and the invitation will be heard for the contemporary life.

Will the Samaritan woman accept Jesus' invitation to new life? "Sir," she says to Jesus, "give me this water, so that I may never be thirsty or have to keep coming here to draw water" (v. 15). The Samaritan woman's initial words to Jesus indicate that perhaps she has indeed heard him, that she understands the promise and power of living water. She requests water from Jesus, just as he anticipated in v. 10, but the transformation Jesus envisioned for her is incomplete. Her final words in v. 15, that she may not "keep coming here to draw," indicate that she is still concerned with miraculous drinking water and not with living water that makes available the presence of God. The woman understands the offer of water to be related to a particular well or spring rather than to the person and presence of Jesus. Nicodemus could not comprehend what it meant to be born *anothen* because he could not move beyond the physiological limitations of his mother's womb. So, too, the Samaritan woman cannot comprehend living water because she cannot move beyond the familiar wells and water jars. In one important respect, however, the Samaritan woman has moved beyond Nicodemus. Even though she does not fully understand, she shows that she is open to Jesus' invitation and asks him to give to her.

The request for water in v. 15 brings the first half of the conversation between Jesus and the Samaritan woman to a close. Verse 10 sets the task for this first half: "If you knew…you would have asked," and the Samaritan woman has asked, but she has asked without knowing who Jesus is and the full scope of his invitation. When Jesus speaks to the woman again in v. 16, it will no longer be about living water. He will turn the conversation in a new direction and speak to her about her own life experience.

Verses 16–26

Verses 16–19 have received the most controversial treatment of any of the sections of this long chapter. The majority of interpreters, scholars and preachers alike, tend to focus almost single-mindedly on the woman's "sinfulness" and her "shady past."[5] Such interpretations, however, do a great disservice to this dialogue between Jesus and the Samaritan woman. When we read vv. 16–19 carefully, we notice that the history of the woman's five husbands is presented quite disinterestedly, with no suggestion or coloring of moral outrage or judgment. How or why the woman has had five husbands and the quality of those marriages are not a concern of the Evangelist as he tells the story. More importantly, those questions are also unimportant to Jesus. One searches in vain for any words of judgment about the woman's character uttered by Jesus in these verses. This exchange between Jesus and the Samaritan woman is not an attempt to bring the woman face-to-face with her sinfulness or to place her in a posture of confession before Jesus. To see the text in this way is to miss the main function of the exchange. The conversation of vv. 16–19 is intended to show the reader something about Jesus, not primarily about the woman.

The ease with which preachers preach sermons about the sinfulness of the Samaritan woman demonstrates the way all readers bring preconceived categories and assumptions to the interpretation of biblical texts and the impact those preconceptions have on what we are able to discover in a biblical text. When the Samaritan woman is characterized as a "loose woman," for example, the interpreter is projecting onto the story what he or she thinks should be there, even when it is not. Not only do such interpretive projections alter the story by focusing on what is not present, they also make it difficult for the interpreter to receive the word of good news that actually is offered by the text. As noted in an earlier context, the particulars of a text matter, and the surprising places where the good news may reside will be lost to the interpreter when he or she does not take care in attending to the details. This is the reason that biblical scholars stress the importance of the exegetical disciplines: not

---

[5]A blatant example of this approach to vv. 16–19 is found in Duke, *Irony in the Fourth Gospel*. Duke refers to the woman as a "five-time loser" (102) and a "tramp" (103).

because only experts can interpret biblical texts, but because the rigor of disciplined exegetical work safeguards that each word and verse of a biblical text is read carefully. In that way, we have a chance of encountering the voice of the biblical text in all its fullness. If our expectations of what a text will or should say preclude us from a fresh engagement with it, then we are the same as Nicodemus, whose expectations about birth precluded his embrace of Jesus' offer, or as the Samaritan woman, whose expectations about water almost caused her to miss Jesus' offer of new life.

The second half of the conversation opens with another request by Jesus. In v. 7 he asked for a drink; now he asks the woman to summon her husband and return to the well (v. 16). The woman did not comply with Jesus' first request because it was impossible according to her customs and conventions. She does not comply with Jesus' second request either, because it, too, is "impossible." She has no husband (v. 17). Jesus, as we have seen already in John 3, does not take impossibilities at face value, however. He takes the woman's refusal and turns it back on her: "You are right in saying, 'I have no husband'; for you have had five husbands, and the one you have now is not your husband. What you have said is true!" (vv. 17–18).

Jesus begins and ends his speech by asserting that the woman has spoken truthfully. Yet within the frame of these two affirmations, Jesus places the woman's "truthful" statement in an unexpected context. Jesus has been able to penetrate beyond the surface level of the woman's words and arrive at the truth about the woman's life. Jesus moves beyond the conventional reading of "I have no husband" to its surprising truth. For the woman and the reader, Jesus' ability to see and to know is stunning. Jesus' perception is stunning to the woman because Jesus has seen through her understatement to the truth. Jesus' perception is stunning to the reader because the reader had accepted the woman's words at their conventional face value and had no hint of the surprising truth uncovered by Jesus. The woman has indeed spoken the truth, but the reader is unable to discover the full range of that truth without Jesus' assistance.

It is no wonder, then, that Jesus' insight into the woman's words and life leads her to declare him to be a prophet (v. 19). The woman's response recalls the response of Nathanael in 1:47–49. Jesus recognizes Nathanael as "an Israelite in whom there is no deceit," simply by virtue of having seen Nathanael under the fig tree. Jesus' recognition of him leads Nathanael to declare Jesus to be the Son of God and the King of Israel. With both Nathanael and the Samaritan woman, Jesus' demonstration of perception and insight leads to increased perception and insight about Jesus' identity on the part of his conversation partners. An important difference between the two scenes, however, is that the reader can only observe Jesus' demonstration of knowledge with Nathanael (cf. also the passive role of the reader in 2:23–25), whereas in 4:16–19 the reader experiences the unveiling of that knowledge for himself or herself. The reader shares with the woman the experience of Jesus' ability to know hidden truths.[6]

Now that the Samaritan woman has recognized Jesus as a prophet, she takes the lead in moving the conversation in an explicitly religious direction. The Samaritan woman seems to debate Jesus about Samaritan/ Jewish relations: "Our ancestors worshiped on this mountain, but you (second person plural pronoun, so "your people" is implied) say that the place where people must worship is in Jerusalem" (v. 20). In one sense the woman returns to her initial comment of v. 9, which also focused on the relationship between Samaritans and Jews. She is no longer concerned only with social propriety, however. Instead she moves to the heart of the religious divide with someone she perceives to be a prophet.

---

[6]Gail R. O'Day, "Narrative Mode and Theological Claim: A Study in the Fourth Gospel," *Journal of Biblical Literature* 105 (1986): 657–68.

This move on the woman's part is not, as is frequently argued, an act of distancing, an effort to extricate herself from an embarrassing conversation about her marital history. Such a view of vv. 20–26 is based on a misperception of the function of vv. 16–19 and on an excessive devaluation of the woman as a legitimate conversation partner.[7] Verses 16–19 do not have as their focus the personal history of the Samaritan woman. Rather, this piece of conversation has as its focus the revelation of the prophetic dimension of Jesus' identity. By engaging Jesus about the proper place of worship, the woman is not distancing herself from Jesus because she is afraid to have her "sinfulness" probed more deeply. Rather, her interest in worship is a commendable act of engagement with Jesus, because she anticipates that Jesus, as a prophet, will be able to speak an authoritative word. It is a level of engagement that Nicodemus never reached in John 3. In acknowledging Jesus as a prophet and turning to him for instruction, the Samaritan woman takes a decisive step toward fulfilling Jesus' invitation of v. 10 ("If you knew...you would ask").

The Samaritan woman frames her observation about worship in the traditional language of her religious practice—our ancestors (Samaritans) vs. you (the Jewish people), this mountain (Gerizim) vs. Jerusalem. Jesus' opening words in v. 21 show that he, unlike many commentators, does not see her words as disingenuous, but instead enters into conversation around the topic that she has broached ("Woman, believe me, the hour is coming when you will worship the Father neither on this mountain nor in Jerusalem"). Yet his initial comments sound almost like a rebuke, because in v. 22 Jesus criticizes the Samaritan perspective ("You

---

[7]Edwyn Clement Hoskyns, *The Fourth Gospel*, ed. Francis Noel Davey, 2d ed. (London: Faber and Faber, Ltd., 1947), 237, 243, suggests that the woman wants to determine at which sacred place she should pray for forgiveness of her sins that Jesus has brought to light. Duke, *Irony in the Fourth Gospel*, 103, says that the woman tries "desperately" to put distance between herself and Jesus. So also Robert Kysar, *John* (Minneapolis: Augsburg, 1986), 66. Brown, *John (I–XII)*, 176, doubts whether "a Samaritan woman would have been expected to understand even the most basic ideas of the discourse." In all these interpretations, the woman is given very little credit as a legitimate conversation partner for Jesus. For an analysis of this conversation that recognizes the full weight of the woman's role, see Schneiders, *Written that You May Believe*, 126–48.

worship what you do not know") and seems to align himself with the Jewish side of the Samaritan/ Jewish divide ("we worship what we know, for salvation is from the Jews"). As Jesus' remarks proceed, however, it becomes apparent that Jesus is only repeating the traditional Jewish interpretation in order to transcend it. He uses the language of "you" (Samaritan)/"we" (Jews) and "this mountain"/Jerusalem not to confirm tradition—both Samaritan and Jewish—but to move beyond them.

The key to Jesus' transformation of traditional religious categories lies in the phrase "The hour is coming, and is now here" (v. 23; see also the beginning of v. 21). "The hour is coming" is a word of promise and anticipation. The phrase "and is now here" signals that this anticipated time of promise and hope is upon us. Through this impingement of God's full hope, true worship will no longer be defined by place or ethnicity. Instead "true worshipers will worship the Father in spirit and truth, for the Father seeks such as these to worship him. God is spirit, and those who worship him must worship in spirit and truth" (vv. 23–24). Both Gerizim and Jerusalem lose their singular status as holy places, because God's presence will neither be defined nor limited to the sanctuaries circumscribed by these conflicting traditions. Because God is Spirit, God moves freely (cf. John 3:8) and seeks those who worship freely in spirit and truth. The worshipful interrelationship of God and believers is more fundamental than the claims of any tradition to have an exclusive hold on God's presence.

Jesus' words to the woman in vv. 21–24 focus on the power of eschatological newness—the inbreaking of the new age. "Everything old has passed away; see, everything has become new!" (2 Cor. 5:17; cf. also Isa. 43:18–19; 66:22). Jesus' presence in the world changes a word of anticipation—"the hour is coming"— to a word of fulfillment—"and is now here." The Samaritan woman's response in v. 25 indicates that she heard the eschatological promise of Jesus' words: "I know that Messiah is coming" (who is called Christ). "When he comes, he will proclaim all things to us." Jesus speaks of the coming hour; the woman speaks of the coming One.

The critical difference between Jesus' words and the woman's words is that the woman does not seem to grasp the eschatological immediacy so central to vv. 21–24. The woman's words focus on "the hour is coming," but reflect nothing of the "and is now here" of which Jesus speaks. To Jesus' vision of eschatological newness, the Samaritan woman responds with traditional eschatological categories of the future expectation of the Messiah.

In vv. 21–24 Jesus has shown the Samaritan woman a world in which new relations with God are possible, in which worship in spirit and truth is possible. Jesus has invited the woman to enter a world bounded neither by "this mountain" nor Jerusalem, a world determined by the inbreaking of the eschatological hour. Jesus has shown all this to the woman—and yet she still waits. Her view of the world is shaped by what she has been taught by her religious tradition, and she knows that the Messiah is the one for whom she waits. How could he be the one with whom she speaks (cf. v. 10)? She listens carefully to Jesus, and he and she both speak about the coming of God's new age, but nothing in her experience has prepared her to embrace the present moment as that new age.

Jesus' response to the Samaritan woman's traditional affirmations about the future and the Messiah is simple and bold, "I am, the one talking to you" (v. 26; auth. trans.). Translations of Jesus' words here downplay the boldness of Jesus' remarks by supplying a predicate ("he"), which is not present in the Greek for the *ego eimi* saying. For example, the NRSV of this verse reads, "I am he, the one who is speaking to you," and the NIV reads, "I who speak to you am he." When the predicate is supplied, the meaning of Jesus' words becomes, "I am the Messiah you expect." Such a translation, however, is more in line with the Samaritan woman's flawed understanding of Jesus than with Jesus' own announcement, because to translate *ego eimi* as "I am he" is to reduce Jesus' words to an assent to the woman's Messianic expectations. This translation loses the boldness of Jesus' announcement, because when Jesus speaks the "I am" in v. 26, his words make explicit connections with the divine name of Exodus 3:14 ("God said to Moses, 'I AM WHO I AM'"). Jesus speaks the "I AM" without any predicate supplied in order to evoke the fullness of God's presence and to identify himself as the one in whom God can be found.[8] The "I AM" places in Jesus' own mouth the theological truth with which the Fourth Evangelist begins the gospel: "In the beginning was the Word, and the Word was with God, and the Word was God." Jesus will spell out the meaning of "I AM" in 10:30: "The Father and I are one."

Jesus' words to the Samaritan woman in v. 26 are yet another promise and challenge. She accepted Jesus as a prophet (v. 19) and anticipated a future Messiah (v. 25). Jesus proclaims to her that the very one with whom she speaks is the one who is able to pronounce the "I AM," the one whose true identity is known through his relationship with God. Nothing in her tradition could have prepared her for the radical power of Jesus' self-revelation. No prior words in this text have had such an impact and force as the "I AM," nor have any other words been spoken so directly. In vv. 10, 13–14, Jesus invited the woman to accept his offer of living water and new life, but the invitation was somewhat indirect, couched in irony, wordplay, and misunderstanding. At v. 26, all indirection is cast aside. The fullness of Jesus' identity is revealed to the Samaritan woman. Will she now accept the offer of new life?

The conversation between Jesus and the Samaritan woman ends on a note of dramatic intensity: Jesus has just made the fullest revelation of his identity to this point in the gospel story. He and the Samaritan woman have moved together from a beginning point shaped by puzzlement and doubt (v. 9) to a full conversation about the nature of God and relationship with God. The Samaritan woman has held her own with Jesus, recognizing

---

[8]Other absolute uses of the "I AM" saying (without a predicate) include Jn. 6:20; 8:24, 28, 58; 13:19; 18:6.

the eschatological promise in his words, and voicing her own eschatological hopes to him (v. 25). In response to her expression of hope, Jesus reveals himself as the embodied presence of God ("I AM"). The impact of Jesus' words on the woman is not immediately narrated, thus heightening the dramatic intensity of the moment.

Transition: Return of the Disciples and Departure of the Woman (4:27–30)

While Jesus is still conversing with the Samaritan woman, the disciples return from the city, where they had gone to get food (see v. 8). That Jesus would converse with a strange woman in public contradicts all the social conventions to which the disciples are accustomed, and their response is astonishment. Yet the disciples keep their reaction to themselves (v. 27); they do not voice their questions to Jesus. This is in marked contrast to the Samaritan woman, who asked Jesus directly about his behavior when she thought that it contradicted social convention (v. 9). In voicing her question to Jesus, she initiated a conversation that led to the stunning revelation of v. 26. By not engaging Jesus directly, even with questions of amazement and consternation, the disciples seem to foreclose that kind of experience of Jesus. They show themselves to be closer to Nicodemus, who focused on what is not possible, than to the woman, who was willing to listen to Jesus.

After the disciples arrive, the woman departs from the well and returns to the city. When she departs from the well, she leaves her water jar behind (v. 28). On the level of the plot line of John 4, the abandoned water jar provides a connection between Jesus' two conversations at the well. The woman's jar remains on stage while Jesus and his disciples speak. Yet the reference to the water jar may be another instance of multiple levels of meaning in a single narrative detail. It is possible to read the woman's abandoning of her water jar as an indication that she has moved beyond her request for miraculous drinking water in v. 15. She may now recognize that she does not need her water jar in order to receive the gift of living water that Jesus offers.[9]

What is most important about the woman's departure is not that she leaves her water jar, however, but what she does after she departs. She returns to the city and bears witness of Jesus to the Samaritan townspeople: "Come and see a man who told me everything I have ever done! He cannot be the Messiah, can he?" (v. 29). The NRSV translation correctly captures the tone and intent of the woman's question. Her affirmation is somewhat tentative, but it is nonetheless expectant and hope-filled. She is not sure if Jesus fits the categories that she has for "Messiah," but she is filled with enough sense of hope and promise at what she has heard from him that she wants to share her experience. She may not be sure that her name for Jesus is correct, yet she is still moved enough to want to share the news of Jesus with others. She bears witness to Jesus, and as a result of her witness, the townspeople set out to see Jesus themselves (v. 30).

After Jesus' self-revelation to the woman in v. 26, the story does not record the woman's reaction. At this point of dramatic intensity, of wondering "does she get it?" there is only silence as the narrator comments on the disciples' arrival and the woman's departure. The Samaritan woman breaks this silence with her announcement to her townspeople. In a sense, it is a surprising announcement, because the reader has not known how the woman has received Jesus' words of v. 26. In another way, it is not so surprising, because throughout this conversation, she has shown herself to be capable of an ever expanding spirit, able to move and grow with Jesus at each turn in the conversation.

The balance of silence and subsequent surprise is suggestive for the dynamics of preaching this passage. As has been the case

---

[9]See Gail R. O'Day, "The Gospel of John: Introduction, Commentary, and Reflections," in *New Interpreter's Bible,* vol. 9 (Nashville: Abingdon Press, 1995), 569. Sandra Schneiders suggests the woman's abandoning of the water jar is comparable to the actions of the male disciples in the synoptic gospels who abandon their fishing nets to follow Jesus—the setting aside of everyday concerns to enter into discipleship (*Written that You May Believe,* 141).

at many points in the Fourth Gospel, the reader is not simply *told* that the Samaritan woman has grown in faith and understanding, but is *shown* this as a result of moving alongside her through the encounter with Jesus. At many points the contemporary reader and preacher of John 4 may be tempted to take a superior attitude to the woman, able to see the double meaning in Jesus' words before she can, feeling capable of recognizing Jesus sooner than she does. But one takes this attitude at one's own peril, because the Fourth Evangelist has presented us with a character who never ceases to surprise. The answer to Jesus' invitation and challenge in v. 10 ("If you knew") is not a preset confession of Jesus' identity. The Samaritan woman could have relied on the vocabulary of her tradition, "Messiah," to sum up all that Jesus had offered her, but that traditional confession fell flat next to her lived encounter and experience of Jesus. Recognizing the possibility of identifying Jesus as Messiah begins the transformation, but it is the grace with which the experience of Jesus is shared with others that completes it. In preaching this woman's story, then, the preacher is called not to take her words out of her mouth and put them in the preacher's own mouth, but to stand with the congregation on the receiving end of her witness, honoring the grace and surprise of her encounter with Jesus.

Conversation: Jesus and the Disciples (4:31–38)

The story's focus changes with the Samaritan woman's departure in v. 28. The woman has been on center stage, with the disciples offstage looking for food for Jesus. Now the disciples will be on center stage, and the woman will be offstage with the Samaritan townspeople. The movement of the Samaritan townspeople toward Jesus provides the frame (vv. 30, 39) for the conversation between Jesus and his disciples. Jesus' conversation with his disciples follows a pattern similar to his conversation with the Samaritan woman, though in a more abbreviated form. Like the conversation with the Samaritan woman, the conversation with the disciples will be triggered

by a misunderstanding. Jesus will then move from this misunderstanding to a teaching in which he offers a new way to
think about religious experience (cf. his words about worship
in vv. 21–24 and mission in vv. 35–38).[10]

Since the disciples were absent from the scene because they
had gone to look for food, it is logical that they offer Jesus food
upon their return: "Rabbi, eat something" (v. 31). Jesus responds
to their offer of food with the words, "I have food to eat that
you do not know about" (v. 32). This is not the response the
disciples expect, because they had assumed that they were the
only ones that had gone to get food for Jesus, and now it appears
that someone else has brought Jesus food before them. Since the
reader knows that the Samaritan woman never got around even
to giving Jesus a drink of water, the reader, too, may be puzzled
by Jesus' words.

In 4:7–15, the Samaritan woman understood "living water"
to refer to some form of drinking water, and therefore could not
comprehend what Jesus was offering her. The disciples make a
similar mistake here. When Jesus mentions food to eat, the
disciples think he has already had a meal while they were off in
the city, and so are confused. Yet whereas the Samaritan woman
voiced her confusion directly to Jesus, and so opened up a
possibility for conversation, the disciples keep their confusion
to themselves. They ask one another about who might have
brought Jesus food (v. 33), but do not engage Jesus (cf. their
unspoken comments in v. 27). Since they will not initiate
conversation with him, Jesus must take the lead in breaking
through their confusion and misunderstanding.

In his opening words of v. 34 Jesus defines what he means
by food: "My food is to do the will of him who sent me and to
complete his work." The food that sustains Jesus is his vocation
to do God's will and to accomplish God's work. The disciples
think of food in terms of bread and fish that can be purchased

---

[10]For a more detailed discussion of Jesus' conversation with his disciples, see O'Day, "John,"
569–70.

in the city, much as the Samaritan woman thought of living water in terms of springs and water jars. Jesus, however, knows that his food, that which nourishes him, is to do God's will. For him, nourishment comes from what he does, not from what he consumes. Much as he asked the woman to think of the refreshment of living water in a new way, here he asks the disciples to reassess their understanding of nourishment. In the earlier discussion of 4:4, we suggested that the necessity of a trip through Samaria may have been driven by more than geographical practicality. When 4:4 is read alongside 4:34 it is possible to understand Jesus' journey through Samaria and his conversation with the Samaritan woman as his "food," as Jesus' sharing in the work of God through his mission to the Samaritans.

If the disciples can understand food and nourishment in terms of work and vocation, then they will be able to receive the offer of new life. In order to bring them to this new understanding of food, Jesus continues to teach them with a series of agricultural proverbs that are loosely connected to one another (vv. 35–38). The metaphor of the harvest, and in particular of sowing and reaping, unites the various proverbs. The metaphor of food as vocation is expanded to include harvest as a metaphor for mission, as Jesus turns the focus from his own vocation to that of his disciples. That which sustains and feeds is to work for others. As Jesus' food was to complete the work of the one who sent him, the disciples' harvest is to complete the work begun by Jesus. The disciples' vocation is dependent on and derivative from God's work in Jesus (vv. 37–38). The disciples enter into the labor of others who have preceded them, and in that labor, new life is possible.

This section of metaphors of vocation and mission takes on added significance when placed in its narrative context. While Jesus and the disciples are speaking, the Samaritans are coming toward Jesus to see if he indeed could be the Messiah. The Samaritan woman has borne witness to Jesus' word and presence. Her actions and the journey of the Samaritans to Jesus illustrate Jesus' words, "I tell you, look around you, and see how the fields are ripe for harvesting" (v. 35). The disciples had gone into the village, and come back with lunch for Jesus. The Samaritan woman had gone into the same village and found true food for Jesus, a way for Jesus to continue to do God's work. The Samaritan woman has already enacted that which Jesus is in the process of teaching his disciples—that true food, and by extension, true drink, is to share in the work of God.

As a result of her earlier conversation with Jesus, the woman is able to see her life through Jesus' eyes—not only in the limited sense of the exchange about her marital history in vv. 16–19, but in the broader sense of being able to see all the world in which she lives through Jesus' categories. Jesus has to exhort his disciples directly to such clarity of vision (note especially the NIV's vivid translation of v. 35, "open your eyes"), but because the woman has moved with Jesus from confusion to confession, she does not need that exhortation. Her experience with Jesus has already changed the way she views the world.

Conclusion: Jesus and the Samaritan Townspeople (4:39–42)

Verse 39 confirms the value of the woman's work: "Many Samaritans from that city believed in him because of the woman's testimony, 'He told me everything that I have ever done.'" As a result of their openness and belief, they invite Jesus to stay with them, "and he stayed there two days" (v. 40). After Jesus' stay with the Samaritans, "many more believed because of his word" (v. 41). The woman's testimony led some to faith; Jesus' word brings more to faith.

By asking Jesus to come stay with them, the Samaritans fulfill the invitation and challenge that Jesus issued for the Samaritan woman in v. 10. They recognize who Jesus is, and they offer him hospitality. They also receive living water from him. Because of their belief in Jesus and the power of Jesus' own word, traditional constraints on Samaritan/ Jewish relations become immaterial. Why? Because the Samaritans know "that this is truly the Savior of the world" (v. 42). The Samaritan woman had suggested that

Jesus might be the Messiah for whom they were waiting. The Samaritans, when they hear Jesus for themselves, understand that Jesus cannot be labeled according to those traditional categories. Jesus is neither the Messiah the Samaritans expect, nor the Messiah the Jews expect. Jesus is the Savior of the world, and traditional expectations pale in the light of this confession. In announcing Jesus as the Savior of the world, the story confirms the reality of Jesus' eschatological promise to the woman: the hour has indeed come when true worship will be defined neither by "this mountain" nor by Jerusalem. Jesus offers new life possibilities to all. The offer of new life is Jesus' food. The embrace of that offer is our drink.

Conclusion

If a sermon on John 4:5–42 can be informed by the give-and-take between Jesus and the woman, the questions and misunderstanding, the boldness of Jesus, and the tentativeness of the woman and the disciples, then the invitation to new life offered in the text will become an invitation for the congregation as well.[11] The preacher must be careful not to present too readily the resolution of the story, either the "I AM" of v. 26 or the christological confession of v. 42, because it is the rich and often multilayered textures of this text, not a preacher's digested version of them, that create a space in which hearing can occur. When preaching this long and intricate text, it is helpful to keep the words of the Samaritan townspeople in mind, "for we have heard for ourselves" (v. 42). While preachers often focus intently, and with good reason, on what they are going to say in sermons, the Samaritans' words remind the preacher that preaching is equally about hearing. It is the preacher's responsibility to allow all members of the congregation to have the experience of

---

[11]For an example of a sermon informed by the give-and-take of John 4, see Eloise Hally, "Lent III," in Janice M. Bracken et al., *Women of the Word,* ed. Charles D. Hackett (Atlanta: Susan Hunter Publishing, 1985), 37–41.

"hearing for themselves." When that happens, the words of a sermon can function as the Samaritan woman's witness—leading a congregation to make their own witness about their experience of the presence of God in Jesus.

CHAPTER 3

John 9:1–41

Introduction

The lesson for the Fourth Sunday of Lent, Year A, is John 9:1–41, the healing of the man born blind. The lectionary's designation of John 9:1–41 as a discrete unit for preaching is another example of how the lengthy narrative units of the Fourth Gospel do not always accommodate themselves well to the demands of the lectionary (see also Jn. 3 above). The decision to end this story at 9:41 is shaped more by adherence to the external markers of chapter division than by the internal markers of the Johannine text itself. The Fourth Gospel text makes no break at all between 9:41 and 10:1; rather, 9:41 is the opening line in a speech by Jesus that runs through 10:18. In its full gospel context, John 9:1–41 belongs to a scene that does not end until John 10:21 and that culminates in some of Jesus' most important statements in the Fourth Gospel about his identity and mission (e.g., 10:9, 11, 15–18).[1]

The tension between the function of the longer unit of John 9:1—10:21 in the Fourth Gospel and the function of the

---

[1]See Gail R. O'Day, "The Gospel of John: Introduction, Commentary, and Reflections," in *New Interpreter's Bible,* vol. 9 (Nashville: Abingdon Press, 1995), 631–71, for a fuller discussion of the relationship of 9:1–41 to 10:1–21.

shorter unit of John 9:1–41 in the Lenten lectionary is instructive about the ways that liturgical uses of biblical texts shape their meaning. In its context as the lesson for the fourth Sunday of Lent, John 9:1–41 becomes a self-contained story well-suited to the Lenten season, highlighting the deepening of faith, as well as the importance of interrogation about the meaning of faith and response to Jesus. These emphases are clearly present in John 9:1–41, but in the broader context of John 9:1—10:21 may not take on the singular significance that their Lenten context gives them. Interestingly, the conclusion of this longer unit, John 10:1–18, provides lectionary lessons for several Sundays of Easter. The "good shepherd" sayings of these verses are as well-suited to Easter as John 9:1–41 is suited to Lent, but it is always important for the preacher to remember that this division and distribution of the texts may serve the liturgical and preaching needs of the church more than it serves the original narrative function of these units in John's unfolding of the Jesus story.

The plot summary of John 9:1–41 recalls many stories in the synoptic gospels—Jesus restores sight to a blind man (Mt. 9:27–31; 20:29–34; Mk. 8:22–26; 10:46–52; Lk. 18:35–43); a healing by Jesus involves him with the religious authorities in a controversy about Sabbath law (Mt. 12:9–14; Mk. 3:1–6; Lk. 6:6–11). The basic plot elements of this story, however, are the scaffolding on which the rest of John 9:1–41 is built. The simple plot line, that a blind man is healed and subsequently cross-examined and rejected by the Pharisees, reflects neither the complicated dynamics of the gradual dawning of faith in the blind man nor the narrative interplay that leads the reader to reexamine his or her own preconceptions about knowledge and sight. As with the stories of John 3 and John 4, the challenge to preachers and teachers is to remain open to the give-and-take of John 9 so that sermons can be shaped by the fullness of this text and not by the points or lessons that we may be tempted to distill from it (e.g., "The blind man stands for...," "The Pharisees stand for...," "The moral of the story is...").

John 9:1–41 is a carefully constructed story of interlacing narrative and dialogue, and its drama-like structure has been frequently noted. Many interpreters have focused on this chapter as a series of seven scenes, but this seven-scene structure emerges only when John 9:1–41 is read in isolation from chapter 10.[2] When it is read as part of its larger unit, a different structure emerges, one which more closely resembles a common Johannine pattern of miracle/dialogue/discourse by Jesus:[3]

I. The Healing Miracle (9:1–12)
    vv. 1–7: The healing
    vv. 8–12: Immediate response to the healing

II. The Dialogue (9:13–41)
    vv. 13–17: The man born blind and the Pharisees
    vv. 18–23: The blind man's parents and the religious authorities
    vv. 24–34: The man born blind and the Pharisees
    vv. 35–38: Jesus and the man born blind
    vv. 39–41: Jesus and the Pharisees

The pattern is completed with the discourse by Jesus in 10:1–18.

This outline highlights the variety of characters in this story. The neighbors and the man's parents each appear in one scene, whereas the man born blind and the Jewish religious leadership are present in multiple scenes and provide focal points for the reader in the unfolding of the story. The focal role of these characters is heightened by Jesus' extended absence from the story. Jesus is not "on stage" from vv. 8–34. This is Jesus' longest absence anywhere in the Fourth Gospel narrative. Jesus' words and deeds in vv. 2–7 set the remainder of the story in motion, and vv. 8–34 demonstrate the resistance and responsiveness that Jesus evokes. When Jesus reenters the story in vv. 35–41,

---

[2]See, for example, George W. MacRae, *Invitation to John* (Garden City, N.Y.: Image Books, 1966), 124.

[3]O'Day, "John," 631.

those who have resisted Jesus and those who have responded to Jesus are both called to accountability.

The narrative reality of Jesus' prolonged absence in John 9 is important to bear in mind as we move through the text. The focus of John 9 is on the response to Jesus, and Jesus does not need to be physically present for the broad spectrum of reactions to Jesus to be explored by the Fourth Evangelist. Even though Jesus is physically absent, he remains the catalyst for all that takes place. Not one scene goes by in which the focus of attention is not in some way on Jesus. The real subject of the interrogations of vv. 8–34 is Jesus, not the blind man.

The outline of John 9 thus highlights one of the central paradoxes of this story: Jesus is physically absent as the story unfolds, but at the same time is rendered inescapably present through the words of the other characters who converse with one another. The absence of Jesus in much of this story gives it a contemporary relevance, because for the modern reader, Jesus is both absent and present.[4] Jesus is physically absent for the contemporary church, but at the same time is rendered inescapably present through the words of this biblical text. The preaching task is to render Jesus inescapably present through the words of the sermon—to communicate the power of Jesus' presence, even when he is absent.

The Text
The Healing Miracle (9:1–12)

The introductory scene of vv. 1–7 can be broken into two parts: vv. 1–5, which function both as the introduction to the healing and as the prologue to the entire chapter; and vv. 6–7,

---

[4]J. Louis Martyn, *History and Theology in the Fourth Gospel*, 2d ed. (Nashville: Abingdon Press, 1979) has articulated two levels on which John 9 operates. The first level is the witness to a particular event during Jesus' lifetime; the second is the witness to Jesus' "powerful presence" in the particular events experienced by the Johannine church. While Martyn is only concerned with questions of contemporaneity for the gospel's original audience, his recognition that the Evangelist has constructed the story in ways that move the story beyond its own time period to that of the reader is suggestive of the ways in which the story is opened up for other readers as well.

which constitute the healing proper. Verse 1 opens with the observation that "he [Jesus] saw a man blind from birth." The two main characters of the story, Jesus and the blind man, are thus introduced, but the two do not immediately enter into any kind of relationship. Instead, the scene is interrupted by what at first glance appears to be a diversion, as Jesus and his disciples engage in dialogue. The man born blind has no active part in this opening conversation, but it is important to envision him lingering on the edges of the stage as this dialogue takes place.

The conversation between Jesus and his disciples in vv. 2–5 is the first instance of a literary pattern that recurs throughout chapter 9, that of question and answer. Each individual dialogue in chapter 9 is structured around this pattern. The relationship between the question asked and the answer given is an essential element in the dynamics of the story, since the relationship between them is not always what the reader might anticipate. In v. 2 the disciples ask, "Rabbi, who sinned, this man or his parents, that he was born blind?" Jesus answers that neither sinned, but that the man was born blind "so that God's works might be revealed in him." Jesus' answer indicates that the disciples' question is not the right way to see what is before them. The disciples ask about the cause of the blindness; Jesus answers about the purpose.

Jesus' answer to his disciples establishes the context in which the upcoming healing must be understood. If the blindness is understood only as a physical infirmity, visited upon someone who "deserves it," then the presence of God in the healing will be missed or misunderstood. The disciples' question reflects traditional categories of the relationship between suffering and sin. Jesus' answer indicates that these traditional categories are inadequate to comprehend the works of God. The blind man is indeed physically blind. He has been that way from birth, but more is at stake in this healing than the gift of sight. Just as the transformation of water into wine at Cana must be understood as a manifestation of glory that leads to belief (Jn. 2:11), so too must the healing of the blind man be understood. It is an occasion for the manifestation of the presence and power of God that can open the door to faith. Through Jesus' words in vv. 3–5, the reader is told what to look for before the healing miracle takes place.

In addition to establishing the proper context for interpreting the healing miracle, vv. 1–5 also introduce many themes that will reappear, in a variety of forms, throughout the narrative. The themes of blindness, sin, the works of God, the contrast between day and night, and Jesus as the light of the world will be important motifs in the unfolding of the story. In many ways this prologue stands distinct from the rest of chapter 9 (for example, the disciples disappear after these verses), but in other more foundational ways, these opening verses cannot be separated from what follows.

The opening phrase of v. 6 ("When he had said this,") explicitly links Jesus' words with his subsequent actions. After these introductory verses, the story moves on to the actual healing. The narration of the healing itself is lean and terse, especially when compared to Jesus' eloquent words that introduce it. Jesus employs a healing technique associated with folk medicine of the time (see Jesus' use of the same technique in Mk. 7:33; 8:23). Once Jesus has applied the clay to the man's eyes, he sends him away to cleanse his eyes in the pool of Siloam (v. 7). The actual moment when the man gains his sight occurs offstage, with no one to witness it. The offstage location of the healing suggests that the revealing of the works of God may not be located in the physical miracle itself.

The blind man's posture during this healing is noteworthy. In v. 1 the narrator notes that Jesus notices the blind man, but there is no indication that the blind man is aware of Jesus' presence. The blind man's presence is accentuated by the disciples' question regarding him (v. 2), but Jesus' subsequent answer shifts the focus away from the blind man to Jesus and God. With this shift of focus, the blind man recedes out of narrative view. In contrast to most other gospel healing stories (cf. Mk. 5:21–34; 7:24–30; 9:14–29), the blind man does not request the healing, nor does he even speak. The blind man is acted upon and is not an actor in his own healing. The blind man voices neither his need nor his faith as a motivation for Jesus to heal him. Nor does he acknowledge Jesus as a healer. Jesus initiates the healing in v. 6, without having had any conversation with the blind man. The gift of sight is freely given, preceding any response of faith. The healing is an act of grace. Such graciousness may contain a clue in understanding what it means to speak of Jesus' healing as the revealing of God's works (9:3).

Jesus is present in vv. 1–7 until the point when he sends the man away to wash. But importantly, Jesus is not present when the blind man receives his sight. The blind man "washed and came back able to see," but he does not come back to Jesus. The blind man (now the formerly blind man) and Jesus do not encounter each other again until v. 35. Much transpires between this first meeting of Jesus and the blind man, out of which the man receives his sight, and their second and final meeting. In the intervening verses, the focus is on the response to the healing and the healer. The gift of sight to the blind man has an impact on not only the one who receives his sight but also on all who learn of it and come into contact with this blind man who can now see.

The first people that the man born blind comes into contact with after he has received his sight are his neighbors and other members of his local community (vv. 8–12). The neighbors serve as witnesses to the miracle, a typical element of a healing story, but their questions about the healing also anticipate and set the stage for the broader dramatic and theological purposes of the rest of the story.

Much like the disciples in John 4 who return to find Jesus conversing with the Samaritan woman, the neighbors initially keep their questions to themselves, not speaking directly about the occurrence that causes them discomfort. They question each other about the man's identity, "Is this not the man who used to sit and beg?" (v. 8). The question about the man's identity draws a mixed response (v. 9). The miracle that has occurred, the gift of sight to a man born blind, is so radical that those who are confronted by it try to find easy and logical ways to explain it. The first attempt to explain the miracle is to doubt the man's identity, to say that he is not the blind beggar but someone who resembles him. If it is a different man, then there is no miracle, and one's sense of order and propriety is preserved. Just like Jesus with his disciples in John 4, the man answers the questions even though they are not addressed to him. The man has not yet spoken in this story, but he speaks now to announce his identity, "I am [the man]" (v. 9).

Since they can no longer evade the miracle by disputing the man's identity, the neighbors ask a second question that focuses on the healing itself: "Then how were your eyes opened?" (v. 10). The blind man answers this question by retelling the healing of vv. 6–7. The man's recounting of the healing (v. 11) is almost as long as the original narration of the event. Such detail in the man's recounting indicates that even though he was a blind and silent partner during the healing, he was carefully attuned to what was being done to him. The blind man identifies his healer by name ("the man called Jesus"), but the identity of Jesus seems to have no more significance to him than any other detail of the healing.

The neighbors' third and final question does not focus on the man who has been healed, but on Jesus. Their question could also be the reader's question at this point in the narrative: "Where is he?" (v. 12). The man's ignorance of Jesus' whereabouts (v. 12) reinforces Jesus' absence from the story. In contrast to the Pharisees, who figure prominently in the rest of the chapter, the man is quite willing to admit his ignorance. He has been asked a question to which he does not know the answer, and he is free enough to say so. The reader may marvel at his nonchalance with regard to Jesus (cf. Jn. 5:13) or at his lack of thanksgiving (cf. Lk. 17:11–19), but the Fourth Evangelist does not direct the story in those directions. Instead the Evangelist presents the reader with a man who is naive, innocent, and guileless enough to say, "I do not know."

The Dialogue (9:13–41)

Verses 13–17: The man born blind and the Pharisees

As indicated, the neighbors have a double function in this story. They serve as witnesses to the healing, but they also function to advance the movement of the story by bringing the man to the Pharisees (v. 13). The order of the neighbors' world has been disrupted—a blind man who used to sit on their streets and beg now sees and converses with them, and so they turn to those who sit in authority to make sense out of the disorder.

Verses 13–17 comprise the first of three successive scenes in which the Jewish religious authorities have a lead role—two with the formerly blind man and one with his parents (see outline). In the first two scenes, their role is clearly that of interrogator, but the shape of that interrogation changes by their second conversation with the man born blind. In the first conversation with the man, the Pharisees continue the questioning that the neighbors have begun. Like the neighbors, they ask how he received his sight. The man's answer is more abbreviated than his response to his neighbors, however, trimmed down to the essentials (v. 15). Nothing more is offered than the minimum required to answer the Pharisees' question.

After the man has responded, the Pharisees ask questions among themselves (v. 16). Sabbath violation, which had been alluded to in v. 14, takes on increased significance as the Pharisees question the healing (v. 16). When Jesus kneaded his saliva into the dirt to make mud (v. 6), he engaged in a type of work (kneading) that was forbidden on the Sabbath. For some of the Pharisees, that violation of religious law is the determining factor as they assess Jesus (v. 16a). For other Pharisees, though, the signs that Jesus has performed seem to be the determining factor, his miraculous acts rendering the traditional category of "sinner" irrelevant (v. 16b). These questions show that there was not a monolithic reaction to Jesus by the religious authorities. They also show the extent of the religious crisis that Jesus' works presented the authorities.

The Pharisees' questions also point to an important difference between the reactions of the neighbors and the Pharisees. The neighbors were divided over the blind man's identity; the Pharisees are divided over Jesus' identity and whether or not he is from God (cf. 3:2). The Pharisees' questions begin with the healing itself, but then move almost immediately to Jesus. This shift is evident in their last question in this conversation with the man, "What do you say about him? It was your eyes he opened" (v. 17).

The man's answer, like his answer to the neighbors' question, is terse and to the point, "He is a prophet" (v. 17; cf. 4:19). The man's innocence and openness are still evident, because he does not equivocate before the religious authorities and try to frame his answer in a way that will please them. He simply tells the truth, regardless of the consequences. The man born blind has moved from referring to Jesus very objectively as "the man called Jesus" to identifying him as a prophet. The man's growing awareness of the truth of Jesus' identity suggests that sight and insight are defined by more or other than physical sight. His physical sight was immediate, but his insight dawns gradually.

The neighbors and the Pharisees have asked three questions concerning Jesus:

Where is he? (v. 12)

How did he do it? (vv. 10–15)

Who is he? (v. 17)

It is the last question, the question of Jesus' identity, that takes on the most weight as the story progresses.

Verses 18–23: The blind man's parents and the religious authorities

In this second interrogation scene, the nomenclature used to describe the religious authorities shifts. In vv. 13–17, the religious authorities are referred to as "the Pharisees." In vv. 18–23, however, they are referred to as "the Jews." Before proceeding to an analysis of this section of the story, it is important to examine this shift, its significance for the direction the story now moves, and its implications for contemporary appropriation of this story.

The nomenclature "Pharisee" is the more conventional New Testament designation for one group of religious leaders at the time of Jesus. The Fourth Evangelist uses this conventional designation at many points in the Fourth Gospel (e.g., 1:24; 3:1; 4:1; 7:45), but he also introduces his own term for referring to the Jewish religious authorities, "the Jews" (e.g., 5:10, 16; 7:1; 10:31). At the time of Jesus, the Pharisees were one among many groups, but by the time of the Fourth Evangelist (80–90 C.E.), the Pharisees' successors, the rabbis, were the dominant group of authorities in Judaism, and the Fourth Evangelist uses "the Jews" as a kind of shorthand to refer to these authorities. The shift from "Pharisees" to "the Jews" in v. 18 is therefore much more than a simple name change. "Pharisees" is a term that locates the events that are being narrated in the historical past, the time of Jesus, but "the Jews" is a term that gives the events contemporary relevance for the gospel readers. The authorities with which Jesus struggled were the Pharisees, but the authorities with which the Fourth Evangelist and his readers struggled were "the Jews."

The Fourth Evangelist shifts from "Pharisees" in vv. 13–17 to "the Jews" in vv. 18–23 in order to signal to his readers that the story he is telling is *their* story and has immediate implications for *their* experience. It is not a Jesus story whose only value is as a historical artifact, a piece of information about the distant past, but is a Jesus story whose value also comes from speaking directly to their setting. The community for whom the Fourth Evangelist wrote was a Jewish-Christian community that understood itself to be living over against the dominant religious authorities of its day. The nomenclature "the Jews" in this scene signals this conflict and that Jesus has a word to offer to this conflict. "The Jews" does not refer to the Jewish people in general, since the blind man and his parents were all Jewish. It is of the utmost importance that contemporary use of the gospel's nomenclature maintain this distinction and place this term in its historical setting.

One of the primary theological and pastoral responsibilities of preaching is to make the "old" word fresh and new, to enable a word of scripture that was written for another millennium to speak a fresh word in this new day. That is what the Fourth Evangelist is doing here in John 9:1–41—making the "old" word of a Jesus story speak fresh words to the situation of a community several decades removed from Jesus' time. As he is telling the story of Jesus, the Fourth Evangelist is simultaneously interpreting the word of Jesus for a new community and a new context. Such interpretive activity marks the Fourth Evangelist as an accomplished pastoral theologian as he recreates the word of Jesus for his community.

Yet the very artistry and theological and pastoral acumen that distinguished the Fourth Evangelist's work for his own time and place increases the interpretive burden on the preacher who wants to interpret John for his or her own time and place. The conflicts with Jewish religious authorities, actual or perceived, that characterized the life of the community for which the Fourth Evangelist wrote and that shaped the way he spoke about "the Jews" are not the conflicts or situations of the twenty-first century church. Simply to adopt uncritically the gospel's nomenclature about "the Jews" here (and elsewhere in the gospel) is to do a serious injustice not only to Jewish-Christian relations, but also to the Fourth Evangelist's pastoral work in telling the Jesus story for the situation of his own community.

The challenge for contemporary Christian interpreters of this text is to remember that the gospel's language here reflects an intra-Jewish struggle, and that with the complete separation of church and synagogue—only in its early stages at the time of the Fourth Gospel—the context in which this language made any sense ended. For the twenty-first century church, the closest analogy to the situation of the Johannine community is one of intra-Christian struggle, in which one segment of the Christian community finds itself in conflict with the prevailing views of the religious authorities. Twenty-first century interpreters of scripture, both teachers and preachers, must work to honor the concreteness of the biblical witness alongside the concreteness of their own contemporary situation. To ignore either concreteness is to ignore the core theological reality at the heart of the Fourth Gospel: "The Word became flesh and lived among us" (1:14).

Even understanding the historical context that led to the Fourth Gospel's nomenclature of "the Jews," however, does not really resolve the ethical dilemma that John 9:18–23 and other texts like it pose for the contemporary preacher. As difficult as the question is, one has to ask whether the strategy that the Fourth Evangelist chose to deal with those with whom he struggled was really the best or most effective strategy. In a situation of intense dispute, negative characterization of one's opponents may have seemed like the only alternative, but it is important that the contemporary preacher also look at the costs of such a strategy for the life of the church and its placement of itself in the world.

The second interrogation scene begins on a very negative note, with the statement that "The Jews did not believe that he had been blind and received his sight" (v. 18). The Jewish authorities may be more focused on questions of Jesus' identity than the neighbors are, but the two groups share a common strategy in accommodating the miracle to their known world. If they can discredit the miracle, then the miracle worker can be ignored. The neighbors attempted to discredit the miracle by denying that the man who stood before them seeing was the blind beggar they had known before (v. 9). The Pharisees attempt to discredit the miracle by denying that the man had ever been blind.

In an attempt to settle whether or not this man was ever actually blind, "the Jews" interrogate the man's parents. They ask the man's parents two questions in v. 19:

1. Is this your son, who you say was born blind?
2. How then does he now see?

The very wording in the first question, "who you say was born blind," indicates that the authorities doubt the veracity of that claim. When the Pharisees ask the parents how it is that their son now sees, it is the third time this question has been asked in the narrative (cf. vv. 10, 15). The repeated asking of this question demonstrates to what lengths people will go to deny what stands before them. The Pharisees have heard the answer to this question already, but they refuse to accept it.

Curiously, the parents respond as if they have been asked three questions instead of two. The parents confirm that this man is their son, that he was indeed born blind (v. 20), and that they do not know how he received his sight. The Pharisees' two questions have now been answered, but the parents add another detail: "nor do we know who opened his eyes" (v. 21). Yet no one had asked the parents who had opened their son's eyes! The parents' answer to an unvoiced question reveals precisely the Pharisees' motivation in conducting the interrogation and their real concern: They are interested in Jesus, not the couple's son. The Fourth Evangelist has deftly crafted the parents' response in order to place the narrative focus on the issue of Jesus' identity as healer and revealer of the works of God.

Two aspects of the parents' third answer deserve comment. First, this third answer contradicts the second answer they gave. The parents initially said that they did not know how the blind man received his sight, but then they go on to say that they do not know *who* opened his eyes. Yet their very words suggest that they do know that a healer was involved and that the identity of the healer is an issue. They know more about the healing than they are willing to let on to the Pharisees. When we read in v. 22 about the parents' fear of "the Jews," vv. 20–21 have already demonstrated implicitly how that fear manifests itself in their behavior.

Second, the parents' third answer is important because of its use of the expression "who opened his eyes." The reader, who has witnessed the healing in vv. 6–7, knows that the answer to the question "How were your eyes opened?" is always "Jesus."

Allusion to the opening of the man's eyes, therefore, functions as code language to evoke Jesus' presence (vv. 17, 26, 30; cf. also vv. 10 and 14). Jesus' name may not be named here, but his powerful presence as the one who opens eyes is part of this scene.

The parents' final words to the Pharisees are ironic, given what has immediately preceded this scene. They tell the Pharisees to ask their son himself (vv. 21, 23). The irony is, of course, that the Pharisees have already asked the man, and he has spoken for himself, but the Pharisees have refused to hear. The repetition of the words of v. 21 in v. 23 underscores the irony of the Pharisees' predicament. They questioned the man's parents because they were dissatisfied with the outcome of their interview with the man himself, but the interview with his parents has resolved nothing. And what is worse, it throws the Pharisees right back to where they started—questioning the man born blind.

In vv. 22–23 the Fourth Evangelist inserts commentary that interprets the parents' response for the reader. This commentary, like the nomenclature "the Jews," moves the situation of the reading community into the story line. Excommunication from the synagogue did not arise at the time of Jesus, but derived from later intra-Jewish conflicts after the destruction of the Jerusalem Temple in 70 C.E.[5] By inserting this commentary, the Fourth Evangelist signals to his readers that their own experience is reflected in the experience of the gospel characters.

Verses 24–34: The man born blind and the Pharisees

The man's parents have not provided the means to discredit the healing that the religious authorities had sought, and so they have no alternative but to converse with the man again. This second interview opens with the words: "Give glory to God! We know that this man is a sinner" (v. 24). "Give glory to God" is a traditional Jewish oath formula, through which a person is

---

[5]Verse 22 is the critical verse in Martyn's analysis of John 9 *(History and Theology)*. Martyn discusses the threat of being cast out of the synagogue as reflective of the life situation of the Johannine community. See O'Day, "John," 657–58.

enjoined to tell the truth (e.g., Josh. 7:19) or to confess one's sin (e.g., 1 Sam. 6:5, Jer. 13:16) as evidence of one's worship of God. On the surface level, then, the Pharisees are executing their appropriate religious role in making this request of the man. Taken on a second level, however, the words "Give glory to God" are ironic, because from the perspective of the Fourth Evangelist, this is exactly what the man has been doing and will do throughout the conversation—he has spoken the truth, but the religious authorities do not acknowledge his confession.

The real motivation for the Pharisees' request is their knowledge that Jesus is a sinner ("we know"). In this final interview between the Pharisees and the man born blind, the verb *know* plays a pivotal role. Much of the dynamics of the conversation is shaped by who claims knowledge, what they claim to know, who recognizes a lack of knowledge, and who in fact possesses knowledge. The verb *know* in v. 24 is the Greek verb *oida,* as it is throughout chapter 9 (vv. 12, 20, 21 [twice], 24, 25 [twice], 29 [twice], 30, 31). There are two verbs of knowing in Greek, *ginosko* and *oida,* and both occur more frequently in the gospel of John than in any other book of the New Testament: *ginosko,* fifty-seven times; *oida,* eighty-four times. Given this frequency, it is striking that only the verb *oida* appears in chapter 9, never *ginosko*. This statistic takes on even more significance when the etymology of *oida* is taken into account: *oida* is derived from a Greek root for seeing *(id-)*. The Fourth Evangelist's choice of the verb *oida* seems intentional and recalls his use of words with an innate double meaning in John 3. Each time a character says "We/I know," their words simultaneously make a claim to sight, "We/I see." By the very language that the Fourth Evangelist uses to speak of knowledge in chapter 9, he signals the reader that there is a connection between knowledge and sight. The nature of that connection will be revealed as John 9 moves to its conclusion.

The Pharisees' first profession of knowledge/sight in this scene (v. 24) is that they know that "this man" (Jesus) is a sinner. This profession of knowledge is a restatement of v. 16. At v. 16, however, the question of whether or not Jesus is a sinner caused a schism among the Pharisees. The Pharisees are now more confident in what they "know" and there is no longer any divide. The lines are sharply drawn—the Pharisees on one side, Jesus and the man born blind on the other.

The relationship between self-professed claims to knowledge (as that of the Pharisees in v. 24) and the actual possession of knowledge is crucial to understanding how the story of chapter 9 resolves itself. The man born blind responds to the Pharisees' confident "we know" with a statement of both what he knows and does not know: "I do not know whether he is a sinner. One thing I do know, though I was blind, now I see" (v. 25). The man born blind, unlike the Pharisees, is reluctant to make categorical judgments and is willing to say what he does not know. Also unlike the Pharisees, he is willing to accept the facts of his experience and to judge accordingly. His experience is that once he was blind, but now he sees. The predetermined designation of "sinner" has no value to the man; what has value is that he has received his sight. The man born blind will not fall into the trap of judging Jesus according to categories determined by the Pharisees. He will judge Jesus according to the gift Jesus has given.

The man's response triggers another set of questions from the Pharisees: "What did he do to you? How did he open your eyes?" (v. 26). The Pharisees already have asked the man how he received his sight (v. 15) and have also inquired of his parents (v. 19). The man has already answered these questions (v. 15), so the Pharisees' entire line of questioning is repetitious and suggests that they are motivated by something other than the acquisition of information. Given this repetitiveness, the content of the man's response is not surprising ("I have told you already, and you would not listen," v. 27), but his boldness in speaking is. Unlike his parents, who attempt to deflect the authorities' questions, the man born blind recognizes them for what they are, and his forthright response forces the Pharisees' hand ("Why do you want to hear it again? Do you also want to become his disciples?"). The man born blind is no longer a passive recipient of what others do or say to him. Here he takes the initiative and with staged guilelessness turns the tables on the Pharisees. For the first time in these interrogations, the Pharisees are on the receiving end of a question. The Greek of the man's final question indicates that he knows that the Pharisees do not want to be Jesus' disciples (cf. the Samaritan woman's question about Jesus and Jacob at 4:12), so his question seems calculated to taunt them. If we envision this chapter as a mini-play, one can imagine the play's audience cheering as the man born blind refuses to be intimidated by the religious authorities. The fear that governed his parents' response to the authorities does not govern his.

The Fourth Evangelist narrates the Pharisees' response to the man's boldness in the strongest possible terms, "they reviled him" (v. 28). To revile is to offer serious insult (e.g., Acts 23:4), and so with this response, the Pharisees' relationship to the man born blind becomes quite clear. Their words further clarify their position with regard to the man, because they contrast their status as disciples of Moses, faithful teachers of the Mosaic law, with the man's status as a disciple of Jesus. The stark contrast of the Pharisees' words—disciple of Moses/disciple of "this man"—suggest that for them, it is an either/or situation. One must choose between Moses and Jesus. For the Fourth Evangelist and his readers, though, it is a both/and situation—to be a disciple of Jesus is also to be a disciple of Moses.

This contrast is heightened in v. 29: Moses' relationship to God is clear and well-known ("we know that God has spoken to Moses"), but nothing about Jesus' relationship to God is clear ("but as for this man, we do not know"). The Pharisees attempt to secure their position and their authority by stating what they know and do not know, but their assertions actually undercut their position. A recurrent theme in the Fourth Gospel is misunderstanding Jesus' origins (e.g., 1:11; 6:41–42; 7:27). The Pharisees assume that Jesus' origin is simply a matter of geography. Since they know so little about where he is from, they "know" that he cannot possibly have a relationship with God that compares to Moses' relationship with God. Yet for the

Fourth Evangelist and the community for whom he writes, the essential identifying characteristics of Jesus are that he is from above (e.g., 3:31; 6:38; 8:23) and that he is from God (e.g., 3:34; 5:43; 6:46; 7:28–29; 8:42).

In attempting to assert their knowledge in v. 29 (cf. v. 24), the Pharisees actually reveal that they do not see/know. Their ignorance carries additional weight in the unfolding of the story because the Pharisees feel so secure in what they do know that they do not see what they might not know. Verse 29 points to a theme that will receive its clearest articulation in the Pharisees' conversation with Jesus in vv. 39–41: sight and insight depend on much more than an external recognition of the facts. Sight and insight depend on seeing with eyes of faith.

The man's fearlessness continues in vv. 30–33. In these verses the man born blind adopts the Pharisees' categories of knowledge and skillfully uses them to indict the Pharisees. The Pharisees' knowledge has led them to assert that Jesus is a sinner (v. 24), and yet, as the man born blind reminds them, "We know that God does not listen to sinners, but he does listen to one who worships him and obeys his will" (v. 31). The common knowledge ("we know") of which the man born blind speaks is the religious heritage shared by the man and the Pharisees: God does not listen to sinners, but to the righteous and those who fear God (see, e.g., Isa. 1:15; Pss. 66:18; 145:19; Prov. 15:8, 29; Job 35:13). The Pharisees have confidently asserted that "we know" that Jesus is a sinner (vv. 24, 29), but in this verse the man born blind tells them that if they really gave heed to what they should know by virtue of their identity as pious Jews, they would reach a different conclusion. The Pharisees have framed their critique of Jesus by appealing to their religious heritage. The man born blind turns that appeal to heritage so that it points toward Jesus instead of away from him.

The man next confronts the Pharisees with the incomparability of the act of healing that Jesus has performed (v. 32). This unprecedented healing—the opening of the eyes of a man blind from birth—makes sense and indeed, is possible, only if God is the source of the healing (v. 33; cf. 9:16b). Since "we know" that God listens to the righteous and that God must be at work for such a remarkable miracle to take place, then Jesus' works must be of God, not opposed to God. Again, the very logic of what the Pharisees insist they *know* points toward the presence of God in Jesus. With his words to the Pharisees, the man returns the reader to Jesus' opening words in the story—that the blindness existed so that the works of God might be revealed. In his healing, the man born blind has "seen" the works of God of which Jesus spoke and now bears witness to them.

The Pharisees' response to the man in v. 34 also brings chapter 9 full circle. In 9:2, Jesus' disciples inquire whether the man's blindness is a result of his sin. Jesus' answer to the disciples' question in vv. 2–3 indicates that the disciples are operating out of the wrong categories. If they understand the man's blindness to be a result of sin, they will be unable to see the manifestation of God's works in the healing. Now, in 9:34, the Pharisees do the very thing that Jesus urged against: "You were born entirely in sins, and are you trying to teach us?" The Pharisees' final words to the man born blind label him a sinner. They do not see God at work in the miraculous gift of sight. They see only a sinner.

The Pharisees also mock the ability of the man born blind to teach them. How can someone who is a born sinner attempt to teach them, the established religious authorities? The notion that they would be taught by a sinner is incongruous to them, yet in that incongruity lies the truth. The man born blind does teach them (the very length of his speech to them is evidence of that), but the Pharisees refuse to be taught. Despite their assumptions and assertions to the contrary, the Pharisees' official status as teachers has not provided them with access to the truth. The witness of the man born blind provides access to the truth, but the Pharisees will not listen. The Pharisees are so certain that they know, are so formed by their own categories and definitions, that they are not open to what is taking place before them. The man born blind would teach them, but they are closed to his teaching. The Pharisees' final action is therefore sharp and decisive. What the man's parents had feared for themselves (v. 22) comes true for their son: "And they drove him out" (v. 34).

The interrogations of vv. 8–34 were all conducted in Jesus' absence. The focus of these verses becomes the variety of responses that Jesus evokes. All the characters, but in particular the man born blind and the Pharisees, have grappled with the significance of the gift of sight that the man received and the identity of the one who bestowed that gift. In vv. 8–34 Jesus is only indirectly present through the controversy that his act of healing occasions. In the concluding verses of chapter 9 (vv. 35–41), Jesus reenters the story, and both the man born blind and the Pharisees will have conversations with him. Jesus will call the man and the Pharisees to accountability for their reactions to him.

Verses 35–38: Jesus and the man born blind

At the beginning of chapter 9 the man born blind was on the outside because he was blind and a beggar. Now he is on the outside again because the Jewish authorities have driven him out. When he was a blind beggar, Jesus found him and gave him sight. Now, when he is a refugee from home and synagogue, Jesus finds him again (v. 35). The initiative in their relationship still resides with Jesus.

Jesus' first words to the man are, "Do you believe in the Son of Man?" Every character who has approached the man in vv. 8–34 questions him, and now Jesus does the same. The questions and answers of vv. 35–38 are different from all that has preceded, however, because Jesus and the man born blind engage in genuine conversation. Jesus' question is not an act of intimidating interrogation, but an invitation to faith. In traditional Jewish usage, the Son of Man refers to a future figure whose coming will mark the beginning of God's final judgment (e.g., Dan. 7:13). In John, this traditional usage is transformed, so that Jesus is the Son of Man whose eschatological judgment is not simply reserved for the future, but is already underway now (e.g., 3:17–21). Just as Jesus challenges the Samaritan woman with the possibility that the anticipated Messiah is actually already present (4:25–26), so now he challenges the healed man with the possibility that the future judge is already present.[6]

The man's readiness to believe is apparent in his question of v. 36. He does not seem to balk at the possibility that the Son of Man might be present now; he only wants to know who the Son of Man is so that he may indeed believe. The way in which Jesus responds to him is important: "You have seen him, and the one speaking with you is he" (v. 37). As with the Samaritan woman (4:10, 26), Jesus identifies himself in terms particular to his relationship with the healed man, identifying himself with reference to the man's gift of sight and to the conversation in which they are engaged. When the man hears these words of Jesus and understands that Jesus is the Son of Man, his response is immediate and unequivocal, "Lord, I believe" (v. 38).

The openness to faith of the man born blind contrasts sharply with the closed, defended position of the Pharisees. Unlike the Pharisees, who would not believe what they had seen (v. 18), the man does believe what he sees. The man allows his experience of Jesus to transform his categories from "the man called Jesus" to "He is a prophet" to "Lord, I believe." This transformation is evidence of a deepening of the man's gift of sight, as he is able to move from physical sight to spiritual and theological sight. The Pharisees looked at Jesus and the man born blind and saw sin. The man born blind saw the power and presence of God in his gift of sight and recognized Jesus as the one who made that power and presence available. The Pharisees branded the man born blind a sinner and cast him out, but Jesus found him and welcomed him home (cf. 10:3–4). In worshiping Jesus (v. 38), the healed man is acknowledging the presence of God in Jesus and his devotion to that presence. The act of worship completes the man's transformation from blind to

---

[6]O'Day, "John," 660.

sighted, and he disappears from the story (cf. the similar "exit" of Nicodemus in John 3).

Verses 39–41: Jesus and the Pharisees

The whole narrative of chapter 9 has been about sight and blindness, but as v. 39 makes clear, sight and blindness operate on many different levels. On the most obvious level, chapter 9 is about the gift of physical sight to a man born blind, vision to someone who has never seen. This gift of physical sight causes consternation among the neighbors who first meet "the man who had formerly been blind" (v. 13; see also vv. 16, 24) and the Pharisees, so that, as we have seen, much effort is devoted to disproving the physical miracle. The gift of sight to a man born blind is an unprecedented feat (v. 32) and as such challenges the categories by which the neighbors and Pharisees organize their known world. As the neighbors and Pharisees question the legitimacy of the miracle, another level of blindness and sight enters the story line, because these groups of characters have physical sight, but do not allow what they see to reshape what they know must and can only be the case. The healed man does allow what he sees to reshape what he knows, so that in vv. 30–33 he knows that God must be at work in his healing because, "One thing I do know, that though I was blind, now I see" (v. 25). The adaptation of the healed man's words in the hymn "Amazing Grace" are an accurate interpretation of the significance of his words: his experience, which redefines what and how he knows, can only be explained as the grace of God.

In v. 39, Jesus speaks about another level of sight and blindness that stands in contrast to being born blind. This is the level at which physical sight is actually blindness, because one does not allow what one's eyes see to transform what one's mind knows: "I came into this world for judgment so that those who do not see may see, and those who do see may become blind." Because of Jesus' presence in the world, those who are born blind may become sighted, but those who are born sighted may become blind.

John 9:1–38 has repeatedly demonstrated how and why such a transformation occurs, as throughout the story the healed man gains deepening insight and the religious authorities become increasingly obdurate and resistant, to the point that they drive the man out from their midst. The conversation between Jesus and the Pharisees in vv. 40–41 reenacts that transformation in encapsulated form. The NRSV translation perfectly captures the tone of the Pharisees' question to Jesus: "Surely we are not blind, are we?" (v. 40). They expect Jesus to affirm that they are exempt from the pronouncement that he has just made, that they are among those who see, not those who are blind. The Pharisees still assert their sight and their knowledge, even after the story has demonstrated their blindness for the reader. Instead of affirming their sight, however, Jesus indicts their blindness.

Jesus' final words in v. 41 show how much the meaning of blindness and sight, knowledge and ignorance, has been transformed by his presence. He inverts the definition of sin out of which the Pharisees operate by explicitly denying any connection between physical blindness and sin ("If you were blind, you would not have sin"). This remark brings the reader back to vv. 2–3. Chapter 9 opened with the disciples trying to find a connection between the man's blindness and sin. Jesus did not answer the disciples directly then, but he does so now— to look for sin in blindness is to miss the meaning of both sin and blindness. Sin is not defined by the presence of illness (vv. 2, 34), nor by the violation of the law (vv. 16, 24, 29).[7] Rather, sin is defined by resistance that closes one to the presence and works of God in the world. According to this understanding of sin, the man born blind is innocent and truly sighted because he has seen and embraced the presence of God in Jesus. By contrast, the Pharisees, who regularly assert their sight and their infallible knowledge even when they are not able to see what is right in front of them, are the ones who sin ("But now that you say, 'We see,' your sin remains").

---

[7]Ibid., 661, 664–65.

Throughout the story the Pharisees have confidently asserted what they know, even when their "knowledge" conflicts with what they see, and now Jesus turns their words against them. Their indictment of the blind man in v. 34 was that he was born in utter sin, but that becomes their own indictment now. Because they are so sure that they know what counts for knowledge and truth, the Pharisees cannot recognize truth when it stands before them. They, not the blind man, are the ones who sin, because they are not open to the truth, and indeed they actively work to hinder its power and presence. The Pharisees are so sure that they know what there is to know and how one is to know it that they cannot be taught (vv. 27, 34). They are so sure that the categories according to which they understand life are the only viable and possible categories that they cannot see the radical works of God made manifest in the healing of the blind man. The Pharisees are unwilling to risk opening up the categories through which they order life, and as a result, despite their protestations to the contrary, they cannot see and cannot know.

Conclusion

John 9:1–41 ends on a very harsh note. To the partisan first readers of the gospel, who may have understood themselves as living in a situation similar to that of the formerly blind man and his parents—oppressed by religious authorities who did not accept their experience of the presence of God in the world as valid or valuable—this harsh note also contains a note of triumph, since the man's ouster from the Jewish religious community becomes the occasion for him to worship Jesus. As we noted in the Introduction to this chapter, even though Jesus' words in v. 41 are positioned as the end of the lectionary lesson, they are actually the beginning of a discourse that runs from 9:41—10:18. This means that the Fourth Evangelist provides more reflection on the story of the healing of the blind man than the lectionary does. Instead of the strictly negative note with which chapter 9 ends, the denunciation of the Pharisees, chapter 10 makes a positive turn to the kind of leader that Jesus is and the kind of community that he creates.

Even within this story's broader gospel context, however, the twenty-first century preacher must still exercise care in the way he or she appropriates the story for the life of the church. The story is so rich, its characters and dialogue so compelling, that the preacher can very quickly find him- or herself so carried along by the flow of the story that Jesus' words of vv. 39 and 41 become the preacher's own, so that the preacher stands and speaks as the one who indicts others for sin. This is always a temptation for preachers—to position themselves as Jesus in relationship to the sinning or sinful congregation—and this text from John 9 sounds a strong cautionary note against such a preaching practice.

John 9 brings the preacher and the congregation face-to-face with the central questions of how we see and what we know. The answer the text offers is that we will never see and never know unless we open ourselves to the presence of God in Jesus, even if that presence challenges and upends many of the categories by which we define our lives. For the man's neighbors, their sense of the natural order of the world was at risk—how can a blind man now see? For the Pharisees, their sense of how God is known in the world and how God is to be received and recognized in the world was at risk—how can God be present in an act that violates the core teachings (sabbath law) of the tradition? For a twenty-first century preacher confidently to point to the neighbors and Pharisees (or even more sweepingly to "the Jews") as "sinners" because of what they do not see or know in this story is to preach *on* this story without having been transformed *by* it.

The danger for the twenty-first century Christian preacher of this story is the same as it was for the Pharisees in the story—to be so sure of what one knows that one is unable to be open to any newness from God. For the Pharisees, their certitude was about the nature of God and the shape of religious life, and for contemporary Christians, the certitude is along the same lines. This text challenges the preacher to be open to unexpected places where God in Jesus may be present and available, to look beyond what one is convinced one knows to see what may be newly possible. Our preconceived categories and our well-defended territory may bring us comfort and security, but they will not lead to knowledge and sight, to healing and life. Unless we are willing to allow the experience of Jesus available in this text to redefine who we are and what categories and labels we use, the contemporary church will be no different from the Pharisees in this story—blind and alienated from the one source of life.

The task of preaching this text is not merely to tell the congregation what the story is "about." The task of preaching is more specifically to enable the congregation to experience what this text does, so that they can experience the move from blindness to sight. As our exegesis of John 9 has demonstrated, this chapter is not a static presentation, but is a story built on intricate dynamics and interrelationships. When we enable our hearers to enter into those rich dynamics, we are faithfully preaching this text. The task of preaching John 9 is not an easy one, given the length and narrative complexity of this chapter. Yet the very things that make preaching John 9 a challenge also make it richly promising. If we allow the mode in which John 9 speaks, with its finely drawn characters, its precisely demarcated scenes, and its animated dialogues, to inform our mode of preaching, then our sermon will do for the congregation what this text does for its readers. It will make present, through the power of the word, the Jesus who gives sight to the blind and who evokes decision and transformation.

CHAPTER 4

John 11:1–45

Introduction

John 11:1–45 provides the gospel lesson for the fifth and last Sunday of Lent, Year A, Revised Common Lectionary. This story, commonly known as the raising of Lazarus, provides an appropriate conclusion both to the season of Lent and to the three Johannine lessons that have preceded it. Those three stories—Jesus in conversation with Nicodemus (Jn. 3), Jesus in conversation with the Samaritan woman (Jn. 4), and Jesus' healing of the man born blind (Jn. 9)—have provided the gospel reader and the worshiping congregation with opportunities to experience for themselves the new possibilities that Jesus offers. The stories have presented a wide spectrum of characters who have responded quite differently to Jesus—from the inquiring caution of Nicodemus to the inquiring openness of the Samaritan woman, from the worshipful acceptance of the man born blind to the skeptical rejection by the Pharisees. Each of these stories has provided the Lenten congregation with the opportunity to experience each of these different responses for itself, because these stories *show* rather than simply *tell* of the challenges and possibilities that arise from encountering Jesus. As the Lenten congregation arrives at the story of John 11, it has seen both responsiveness and resistance to Jesus, and has experienced glimpses of the radical newness that Jesus reveals. In the story of the raising of Lazarus, the text for the last Sunday prior to Holy Week, the gift of life that Jesus offers is now fully visible, in all its grace and glory (11:4). The sequence of Fourth Gospel texts on the second, third, fourth, and fifth Sundays of Lent provides a rich opportunity for the worshiping congregation to move toward Easter with a full picture of the transformative power and presence of Jesus before it.

As with the other lessons that we have examined, the lectionary's designation of John 11:1–45 as a discrete unit partially disrupts the literary strategy of the Fourth Gospel. John 11:1–45 is the first of three units that together tell the story of the raising of Lazarus and its aftermath: (1) 11:1–45, the raising of Lazarus; (2) 11:46–54, the decision to kill Jesus; (3) 11:55—12:11, Jesus' anointing at Bethany. These three units are intimately interconnected, because the raising of Lazarus is presented as the precipitating factor in the decision to kill Jesus, and Jesus' anointing occurs in Lazarus's home, with the raised Lazarus in attendance and his sister Mary doing the anointing. There is a certain logic to ending the first unit with v. 45, because it provides the attestation to the miracle (its corroboration by others) that is a traditional part of telling a miracle story. Yet ending the story on the positive note of v. 45 also makes the Lazarus story too easy and alters its theological voice. As we shall see, the raising of Lazarus is not simply a joyous story of the triumph of life over death; it is also a story of the cost of that triumph. Both of those elements make the Lazarus story the appropriate transition story from Lent to Holy Week and Easter.

John 11:1–45 is the longest sustained narrative in the Fourth Gospel outside of the passion account. The plot of the story is rather straightforward: Jesus hears of Lazarus's illness; Jesus proceeds to the tomb; Jesus raises Lazarus. This plot recalls the stories in the other gospels of Jesus' raising someone from the dead (Mk. 5:21–43 and par.; Lk. 7:11–17, 22; Mt. 11:5). Once again, however, as with the other stories we have studied, such a simple plot summary does not begin to approximate the complexity of the text. The summary plot line of John 11:1–45 does not indicate where this story places its emphasis, where it lingers, where it moves on without a backward glance. As the following analysis of John 11 will show, the text does not always linger where the reader thinks it should linger, nor does it move on when the reader thinks it should move on. When preaching this long text, then, it is important not to rush immediately to what the preacher thinks the story is "about," but instead to allow one's movement through this text to be governed by the way in which the story itself unfolds.

John 11:1–45 has a more complex structure than any of the other Lenten lessons. In discussing the structure of John 9, we noted that in the common Johannine pattern for recounting a miracle story, the miracle (e.g., 5:1–9; 6:1–14; 9:6–7) is followed by a dialogue (5:11–18; 6:25–34; 9:8–40), which in turn is followed by a discourse (5:19–47; 6:35–59; 9:41—10:18). In this pattern, the miraculous event occurs first, followed by the conversations that interpret it. John 11:1–45 alters that pattern: the miracle does not occur until the very last moment of the story (vv. 43–45), and is preceded by interpretive conversations. In addition, unlike in John 5, 6, and 9, there is no concluding discourse—all the interpretation comes in Jesus' conversations with Mary and Martha prior to the miracle. In this regard, the literary strategy of John 11:1–45 more closely resembles that of John 4:4–42, in which there is also no discourse by Jesus and all the interpretation lies inside the give-and-take of the conversation.[1] The structure of the story can be outlined as follows:

I. Introduction: Lazarus's Illness and Death 11:1–16

II. Conversations on the Way to the Tomb 11:17–37
    vv. 17–27: Jesus and Martha
    vv. 28–37: Jesus and Mary

III. The Raising of Lazarus 11:38–45

---

[1] See Gail R. O'Day, "The Gospel of John: Introduction, Commentary, and Reflections," in *New Interpreter's Bible,* vol. 9 (Nashville: Abingdon Press, 1995), 681.

The setting of the Lazarus story in the broader context of the Fourth Gospel is also important to note, as this setting has implications for how this text is preached. As noted above, the Lazarus story is the final catalyst that moves the Jewish authorities to act against Jesus (11:46–54). The connection between the raising of Lazarus and the death of Jesus is unique to the Fourth Gospel. Matthew, Mark, and Luke all locate the decisive impetus for Jesus' death within the events of Jesus' final week in Jerusalem (e.g., Mt. 26:1–3; Mk. 11:15–19), with Jesus' actions in the Jerusalem temple as the catalyst for the formal decision to kill him. Critical scholarship continues to debate the relationship between the Lazarus story and the synoptic gospels and between the different traditions of the cause of Jesus' death.[2] Those questions will never be resolved. What matters for our purposes is that the Fourth Evangelist, in striking contrast to the other traditions about Jesus' death, structures the raising of Lazarus as the last act of Jesus' ministry before his Passion. The story of Lazarus is a radical demonstration of God's power for life as manifested in Jesus, and this radical gift of life precipitates Jesus' own death.

The Text
Introduction: Lazarus's Illness and Death (11:1–16)

John 11:1–5 introduces the reader to the members of a family whom Jesus loves: Lazarus and his two sisters, Mary and Martha. Just as chapter 9 opens with an explicit mention of the man blind from birth, chapter 11 opens with an explicit mention of Lazarus's illness (11:1). Reference to Lazarus's illness precedes the names of any of the family members, and the family portrait also closes with a reference to Lazarus and his illness (11:2). The Fourth Evangelist uses a literary framing device in these opening verses to reflect the role that the three family members will play

---

[2]For an overview of the critical discussion of the relation of the Lazarus story to the synoptic tradition, see Raymond Brown, *The Gospel According to John (I–XII)*, vol. 29, *Anchor Bible* (Garden City, N.Y.: Doubleday, 1966), 427–30.

throughout the story: ill Lazarus ⟶ Mary-Martha-Mary ⟵ ill Lazarus. The story is occasioned by Lazarus's illness and reaches its climax in the raising of Lazarus. Between these two pivotal framing events, however, Mary and Martha, in conversation with Jesus, occupy the center of the story.

In v. 2 Mary is identified as the one "who anointed the Lord with perfume and wiped his feet with her hair." Mary's anointing of Jesus is included in the Fourth Gospel, but it is not narrated until chapter 12, after the Lazarus story. Is this anticipatory identification a mistake, a slip on the narrator's part, or does it serve some narrative and theological function? On a tradition-critical level, this anticipatory identification of Mary suggests that the Fourth Evangelist is attempting to orient the reader to who Mary is, that is, which Mary, by identifying her on the basis of the way she is known in the tradition, regardless of where the anointing is narrated in his gospel. We find a similar use of traditional material in John 1. In 1:40 Andrew is identified as Simon Peter's brother, although Peter is not introduced into the story until the next verse.

The anticipatory identification of Mary also has a more important theological function in this narrative. The anointing of Jesus in chapter 12 is explicitly portrayed as a foreshadowing of the preparation of Jesus' body for burial (cf. 12:3, 8; 19:39–40) and an anticipation of the passion.[3] By reminding the reader of Mary's role in the anointing, the Fourth Evangelist draws the passion story into the story of Lazarus. The connection between the Lazarus story and Jesus' death is intentionally suggested by the Fourth Evangelist from the outset of chapter 11, so that John 11 proceeds under the shadow of Jesus' death.

The first action of the story occurs when the two sisters send a message to Jesus (v. 3). The two sisters request nothing specific from Jesus. They merely inform him that Lazarus is ill. Their words are similar to the words that Jesus' mother speaks to him at the wedding in Cana. In that story, Jesus' mother informs him

---

[3]See discussion of John 12:1–8 in O'Day, "John," 700–703.

that there is no wine (2:3), but makes no explicit demand of Jesus. In both instances, however, the reader senses that even though the women ask nothing of Jesus, they address him because they expect him to know what to do. The sisters' message to Jesus marks the third time in these opening verses that the reader hears that Lazarus is ill.

Jesus' response to the sisters' message opens with the story's fourth reference to Lazarus's illness, but Jesus' words turn the focus from Lazarus's illness per se to what Lazarus's illness says about the presence of God. Just as 9:3–5 was critical for establishing the interpretive lens through which to see the healing of chapter 9, so now Jesus' response in 11:4 provides the lens for interpreting in advance the events of the Lazarus narrative. Jesus' opening words point toward the end of the story ("This illness does not lead to death"), by anticipating the life-giving miracle with which the story will close. In addition, Jesus' words indicate that this life-giving miracle will reveal the glory of God. The reader of the Fourth Gospel has already experienced a connection between the working of miracles and God's glory (2:11; 9:3), and 11:4 enables the reader to place the raising of Lazarus in that broader context of the manifestation of God in the works of Jesus.

Most importantly, Jesus connects Lazarus's illness and the manifestation of God's glory with the glorification of the Son of God. In 13:31 Jesus will explicitly link the hour of his death with the hour of his glorification, and he anticipates that connection here (cf. also 12:27–32). The allusion to the anointing in 11:2 hinted at a connection between the Lazarus story and Jesus' own death; 11:4 makes that connection unavoidable. Lazarus's illness will not result in Lazarus's death, but it will instead result in Jesus' death and glorification.

Interestingly, the text does not indicate any specific audience for Jesus' words in 11:4. He obviously is not speaking to the sisters, as they have sent a message to him, nor has the text yet mentioned that his disciples are present. Rather, the narrator positions Jesus' words so that the reader of the gospel is included as the immediate audience for the remarks to the same degree that the characters in the story might be. His words move beyond the confines of the story to address the reader and to challenge the reader with the same things that will soon confront Mary, Martha, and his disciples: to experience the illness, death, and raising of Lazarus according to the categories Jesus establishes in v. 4 and not by any preconceptions we might bring to the story. Given the connection Jesus makes between the Lazarus miracle and his own death, the story seems to be signaling very early on the dangers of any appropriation of the Lazarus story that celebrates the glory of God without recognizing that the ultimate shape of that glory is determined by Jesus' gift of his life in his death.

At the end of v. 4, then, the characters have been introduced and the scene set. The reader anticipates some action, some gesture on Jesus' part in response to the sisters' message. Convention dictates that Jesus would go to help those whom he loves (v. 5), yet Jesus stays away longer (v. 6). The juxtaposition of vv. 5 and 6 is jarring. Jesus' actions contradict the conventional dictates of logic, as they have throughout the Fourth Gospel. He told his mother that the wine supply was none of his concern, but then he transformed water into wine anyway (2:3–8). His brothers insisted that he go up to Jerusalem for the Feast of Tabernacles. Jesus refused them, but then he went up anyway (7:1–10). Jesus cannot be controlled even by those closest to him, by his family and friends whom he loves. Jesus will deal with Lazarus, but that he stays away two days longer indicates that Jesus' actions will come at the time he knows to be most fitting. At this juncture in the narrative, Jesus alone understands that Lazarus's illness is for the glory of God. His actions must be understood as proceeding from that awareness, and so cannot be assessed according to behavioral norms of what we would do if someone we loved were ill.

When Jesus deems it to be the appropriate moment, he initiates the movement toward Lazarus (v. 7). Verse 7 is the first indication that Jesus' disciples accompany him; prior to this verse, the focus has been exclusively on Jesus and the family from Bethany. Judea is not a safe haven for Jesus. Jesus and his disciples are outside of Judea (10:40) because the religious authorities in Jerusalem have tried to stone him (10:31). His disciples remind him of the authorities' attempt to kill him and question why he would willingly place himself again within their reach (11:8). The disciples' question, like vv. 2 and 4, explicitly reminds the reader that this story takes place under the shadow of Jesus' death.

Jesus answers his disciples with a metaphor about day and night. His reference to the number of hours in the day indicates that he is not hesitant about meeting his death. Verses 9–10 consist of two parallel sentences, the first positive in meaning (walk during the day, do not stumble); the second negative (walk at night, stumble). The link between the two sentences is the light metaphor. On one level, the day and night imagery can be read so that "the light of this world" refers to the sun, the light that distinguishes day from night and provides the light by which one can work. On this level, Jesus' words sound like a conventional proverb about day and night.

The light metaphor has a broader range of possibilities for the reader of the Fourth Gospel, however. In the gospel prologue, the Fourth Evangelist uses the images of light and darkness to describe the conflicted relationship between Jesus and the world (1:5, 10). Throughout the gospel narrative, language of light and darkness is used to represent the consequences of one's acceptance or rejection of Jesus (cf. 3:19–21). As noted earlier, it is significant that Nicodemus came to Jesus "by night" (3:2). The light imagery reaches a climax in 8:12 and 9:5, when Jesus identifies himself as the light of the world. The reader of the Fourth Gospel brings all these associations to 11:9–10 and is therefore able to discern that Jesus speaks about more than merely the sun here. He speaks about himself and the ways in which his presence and the acceptance of his presence are the ultimate criteria in distinguishing day from night (cf. 12:35–36).

There are important similarities between Jesus' words to his disciples that introduce the healing of the blind man (9:3–5) and his introductory words to his disciples here. In both stories Jesus raises the question of light and darkness, of acceptance and rejection. In both Jesus answers a specific question about one particular event with words that set what is to come in a broader theological context. Both miracles are events that reveal God and God's dealings with the world.

Verses 11–12 are an extended wordplay on Lazarus's death, similar to the wordplays Jesus uses in conversation with Nicodemus and with the Samaritan woman. Up to this point in the narrative, Jesus and the reader know that Lazarus is ill, but the disciples do not possess that knowledge. When Jesus does tell his disciples about Lazarus, however, he introduces a new word to describe Lazarus's condition. Instead of repeating that Lazarus is "ill," which has been the only description of Lazarus to this point, Jesus says that Lazarus has fallen asleep, *koimaomai* (v. 11). Like the words *anothen* ("from above"/ "anew"), *pneuma* ("wind"/ "spirit"), and *hupsoo* ("exalt"/ "lift up") in John 3 that have innate double meanings, *koimaomai* also is a word with a double meaning. It may simply mean "sleep," but it is also used regularly in the New Testament as a euphemism for death (e.g., Mt. 27:52; 1 Cor. 7:39; 11:30; 1 Thess. 4:13–15), similar to the meaning of "sleep" in English language usage. Jesus heightens this wordplay by saying that he must go to Judea to "awaken him." The logical way to read those words, as his disciples do (v. 12), is that Jesus wants to go to Judea to rouse Lazarus from a nap.

The reader has a better chance of deciphering the double meaning in Jesus' words, because the reader, unlike the disciples, knows that Lazarus is ill. Yet even for the reader, there is a surprise in Jesus' words, because Lazarus's death has not previously been reported. For the disciples, though, Jesus' wordplay is impenetrable.

Their response, which clearly does not understand sleep as referring to death, contains its own inadvertent play on words. Its full meaning can be grasped by the reader, but not by the disciples themselves. The disciples do not understand why Jesus would risk death in Judea simply because Lazarus sleeps, because if "he has fallen asleep, he will be all right" (v. 12). The verb that the NRSV translates as "be all right" is the future passive of the Greek verb *sozo*, "to save." In relation to illness, the passive of *sozo* means "be restored to health," "be all right," but other connotations of the verb cannot be categorically excluded. In many of the healing stories of the gospels, the sense of *sozo* as "save" or "deliver" frequently overlays its meaning as "be all right" (cf. Mark 5:28, 34; 10:52),[4] and that double meaning seems at play in this verse as well. That Lazarus will recover, that Lazarus will be restored or saved, means more in the context of this story than the disciples know.

The narrator interrupts the story in v. 13 to make explicit what the reader already knows—Jesus and the disciples are conducting their conversation on two different levels. After the narrator speaks to the reader, Jesus speaks to his disciples: "Then Jesus told them plainly, 'Lazarus is dead.'" Unlike John 4, where Jesus allows the woman to linger in her misunderstanding, here Jesus resolves the misunderstanding almost as soon as it arises by stating quite clearly and boldly that Lazarus is dead. The reader and the disciples are now back on even footing, yet still Jesus alone understands the real significance of Lazarus's death: that it is for the glory of God (11:4).

Jesus' words in v. 15 provide an explanation for the delay in returning to Lazarus. Jesus did not stay away from Lazarus because he was indifferent, but so that the disciples might believe. Verse 15 connects with v. 4, and brings the glory of God back into focus (cf. 2:11, where the manifestation of glory in a miracle is also an occasion for the disciples to believe). Jesus' words do not necessarily satisfy the reader of this story, whose focus remains on Lazarus and the family's grief, so that Jesus' delay appears to be indifference at best, manipulation at worst. Jesus' actions will never satisfy if we read them according to what we

---

[4]Donald Senior, C.P., *The Passion of Jesus in the Gospel of Mark* (Wilmington, Del.: Michael Glazier, 1984), 120, makes a similar observation about the use of *sozo* in Mark.

would do in this situation or even what we would demand that Jesus do. As the exchange with the disciples indicates, Jesus risks his own life by returning to Judea to raise Lazarus, so indifference is hardly a factor here. The needs of Lazarus and his sisters and the occasion for the manifestation of God's glory supersede any threat of Judea ("But let us go to him," v. 15). The tension between our perception of what is appropriate and Jesus' perception of what is appropriate needs to linger as the story develops rather than be quickly resolved, because experiencing that tension may lead the reader to new understandings of how the revelation of God in Jesus is received.

The introductory section of the Lazarus story closes in v. 16 with Thomas's words to his fellow disciples, "Let us also go, that we may die with him." It is unclear to whom Thomas refers when he says, "that we may die with him"—Lazarus or Jesus. The deaths of both have been part of the story to this point. Thomas is the paragon of loyalty here, offering to follow Jesus even to the point of the disciples' own death, yet there is an ironic edge to this loyalty, since the whole scope of what lies ahead is unknown even to Jesus' most faithful disciples. Thomas's words are truer than he can yet know.

The preacher may be tempted to skip all of vv. 1–16 as preliminary to the main event, and indeed, in the lectionary cycle for the Episcopal church, vv. 1–16 are indicated as an optional part of the lesson. To skip these verses, however, is to preach a story other than the one that John tells. As we have repeatedly noted, the Fourth Evangelist has taken great pains in these verses to locate the raising of Lazarus in the context of Jesus' impending death. This context is especially important when preaching this story in Lent. In Lent, the congregation is asked to linger with the significance of Jesus' impending death, contemplating the impact of that death on the congregation's life and the life of the world. Verses 1–16 are an important partner in that contemplation, because they too ask the reader to slow down and think about Jesus' death. When vv. 1–16 are ignored, the weight of the story falls on the miracle and the much-beloved teaching of Jesus as the resurrection and the life (11:25), and it becomes very easy for the triumph of resurrection to push the reality and cost of death to the sidelines.

Conversations on the Way to the Tomb (11:17–37)
Verses 17–27: Jesus and Martha

In vv. 17–19 the reader's attention is redirected to the family who have suffered loss and who grieve. The action of this story may have wide-ranging implications (11:4), but its immediate impact is felt by a grieving family. As with the healing of the man born blind, a particular instance of pain or grief becomes the occasion for a manifestation of the glory of God. Both these stories are a reminder of the truth of the incarnation that is at the heart of the Fourth Gospel, "the Word became flesh and lived among us" (1:14). It is in the details of ordinary human life and death that God will be revealed.

Two details of vv. 17–19 fill out the picture of the family's grief. First, the narrator informs the reader that Lazarus has been in his tomb for four days already. Popular Jewish belief held that the soul remained near the body for three days after death and on the fourth day left the body for good,[5] so this detail reinforces the family's loss and the reality of Lazarus's death. Second, Mary and Martha do not mourn alone. Many Jews have come to join them in mourning. The "Jews" of v. 19 are not the "Jews" who were Jesus' antagonists in 9:4, but are Jewish men and women who come to offer their presence in consolation and support to these two Jewish sisters. The family do not mourn alone, because their community mourns with them. Yet the bigger story is not completely subsumed into this family story. The precise description in v. 18 of Bethany's location, with its explicit mention of its proximity to Jerusalem, continues to remind the reader that this story takes place in the shadow of Jesus' death.

---

[5]Andre Neher, *The Exile of the Word* (Philadelphia: The Jewish Publication Society of America, 1981), 24, provides a reflection on this Jewish belief.

The story moves forward against this backdrop of mourning and Lazarus's four-day entombment. What we find next, perhaps to our surprise, is that Jesus still does not proceed directly to Lazarus's tomb. The act of the raising of Lazarus may be the church's focus as it approaches this story, but it is not so singularly the Fourth Evangelist's focus. The family's grief and Lazarus's long entombment do not cause Jesus to rush to the tomb. Instead Jesus lingers with the family, conversing with them. The Fourth Evangelist devotes much time and care in preparation for the raising of Lazarus, so that when Lazarus does walk out of the tomb, the reader will be able to understand the significance of the act and to see the glory of God in that act. The time that the Fourth Evangelist takes in bringing Jesus to Lazarus's tomb contains an important warning for the preacher. The preacher of this text ought not to arrive at Lazarus's tomb any faster than Jesus does.

When word of Jesus' arrival reaches the two sisters, Martha comes to Jesus first (v. 20). The dialogue between Jesus and Martha has much in common with the other Fourth Gospel lessons we have examined, but especially with John 4. As we study the give-and-take between Jesus and Martha in these verses, we frequently hear echoes of Jesus' conversation with the Samaritan woman.

Martha's words to Jesus open with two bold and, on the surface, contradictory statements:

1. "Lord, if you had been here, my brother would not have died" (v. 21).
2. "But even now I know that God will give you whatever you ask of him" (v. 22).

Martha's words combine accusation and affirmation, resignation and expectancy. Her words lament Jesus' absence and perhaps negligence in not coming to Lazarus sooner, while at the same time affirming her faith in Jesus' ability to act. The edge of complaint in v. 21 increases the impact of her statement of confidence in v. 22. Martha's confidence in Jesus is spoken out of the depths of her despair and disappointment. The "even now" of v. 22 suggests that even in the face of death, Jesus will be able to act. Martha's words are a confession of trust in Jesus' power "even now" to mobilize God for good.

In v. 23 Jesus speaks directly to Martha's hopes: "Your brother will rise again." Yet these seemingly straightforward words are actually rich with ambiguity, because Jesus supplies no temporal referent for the resurrection of which he speaks. Martha steps right into this ambiguity (v. 24). She responds to Jesus' words affirmatively and couches her agreement with him in the language of traditional Jewish teachings on the resurrection: "I know that he will rise again in the resurrection on the last day." She has heard Jesus' words as a reference to the traditional teaching about the future general resurrection of the dead.[6] Martha interprets Jesus' words through her own preconceived categories and assumptions, and so is confident that she understands and agrees with what Jesus says about the resurrection. Verses 25 and 26 demonstrate, however, that the distance between Martha's understanding and Jesus' words is great.

Jesus' response to Martha immediately challenges the traditional eschatological categories and expectations out of which she speaks. Jesus, by his presence in the world, has made such traditional categories and expectations obsolete: "I am the resurrection and the life." The victory over death that the resurrection represents is present now, incarnate in the person of Jesus. Jesus, who transforms all categories, here announces that he transforms even categories of life and death. Nothing remains outside the sphere of Jesus' transforming power. By identifying himself as both the resurrection and the life, Jesus identifies himself as lord over the present power of death and the future power of death.

Verses 25b–26a consist of two parallel phrases built around three main verbs: believe, live, and die. In verse 25b, the focus is on the effect that believing in Jesus has on death:

---

[6]This teaching was affirmed by the Pharisees at the time of Jesus, but denied by the Sadducees; see Acts 23:6–8; Mk. 12:18–27.

The one who *believes in me* yet *dies* ⟶ will *live.*

In verse 26a, the balance is reversed, and the focus is on the effect that believing in Jesus has on life:

everyone who *lives* and *believes in me* ⟶ never *dies.*

The fulcrum of both verses, the only piece that remains constant, is the expression "who believes in me." Through the careful symmetry with which they are constructed, vv. 25b and 26a make a radical claim for the power of faith in Jesus: Believing in Jesus transforms death (v. 25b), believing in Jesus transforms life (v. 26a). These verses play out the suggestive language of Jesus' "I am" statement in v. 25a and give body to the ways in which Jesus is the resurrection (v. 25b) and the life (v. 26a). Both the believer's present (v. 26a) and future (v. 25b) are determined by faith in Jesus, so that in life and death, everything is redefined by Jesus.[7]

The importance of believing is highlighted in Jesus' final question to Martha: "Do you believe this?" Verses 25 and 26a make it clear that the question Jesus asks is not idle curiosity, but a fundamental question of life and death. When Jesus asks Martha if she believes, he is asking her whether or not she is to be included among those of whom he has just spoken. He is offering her the chance to have her life transformed.

Martha responds positively to Jesus' question (v. 27), but as with Thomas's remarks in v. 16, it is unclear whether she is aware of the full meaning of what Jesus has said or what she embraces in her affirmation. Her response, like her earlier response in v. 24, is couched in the traditional language of messianic confession (cf. for example, the list of titles used by Jesus' disciples in 1:35–51). As was the case with the Samaritan woman in John 4, it is clear that Martha recognizes in Jesus the Messiah that her tradition has led her to anticipate. What is not

---

[7]See O'Day, "John," 688–89, 694–95.

as clear, especially given her allusion to the future ("the one coming into the world"), is whether she also recognizes how Jesus redefines those expectations. The question of whether or not Martha's confession fully recognizes what Jesus has to offer—that the Messiah is present now, not still at some distance in the future—is not immediately resolved by the story. Once Martha has spoken her confession, she exits the scene (v. 28) and will next appear beside Lazarus's tomb.

In this conversation with Martha, Jesus has presented a theologically rich image of the ways in which who he is redefines expectations of how God is present in the world and of the significance of that redefinition for those who believe. His question to Martha, "Do you believe this?" becomes a question for the worshiping congregation as well. The preacher is invited by this text to allow Jesus' question to linger unanswered for the congregation for a moment. A sermon does not need to move immediately to the certitude of confession ("Yes, Lord, I believe," v. 27), but instead can open up the many ways in which Jesus as the resurrection and the life reshapes the church's most basic perspectives on its life in the world.

Verses 28–37: Jesus and Mary

In v. 28 the focus of attention shifts from Martha to Mary. Martha informs Mary that the "Teacher" is calling for her, and Mary rises and goes "quickly" to Jesus. The story does not "quickly" narrate the meeting between Mary and Jesus, however, but instead the narrative focus shifts from Mary to the Jewish mourners who have been keeping company with her in the house. The mourners follow her, thinking that she is heading to her brother's tomb to weep (v. 31), so that the conversation between Mary and Jesus that follows, unlike Martha's conversation, is not a private conversation, but one witnessed by all Mary's fellow mourners. Just as the community has shared in Mary's grief, they will now be witnesses to the transformation of that grief.

Mary greets Jesus the same way her sister did: "Lord, if you had been here, my brother would not have died" (v. 32). While it has been argued that the exchange between Mary and Jesus does not greatly advance the plot of the story, or is evidence of a secondary level of tradition,[8] in reality, this exchange does open up new perspectives for the gospel reader. There is a certain poignancy in Mary's repetition of her sister's greeting—it continues to lay the family's grief before Jesus so that the particularity of this one family's experience of death does not fade from view. Mary's words express complaint and disappointment that Jesus was not present at the crucial point in Lazarus's illness; her actions—coming when Jesus calls her, kneeling, weeping—embody her continuing confidence and hope in him. And importantly, this combination of despair and hope is not a private communication between Mary and Jesus, but is spoken in front of the group of mourners. The gospel reader and the mourners share the same perspective—witnesses to the intimacy of Mary's devotion to Jesus, even in the face of her brother's death. And importantly, the mourners join her in her weeping (v. 33).

Verses 33–35 are among the most difficult verses to interpret in the entire Fourth Gospel. What is clear is that the weeping of Mary and the Jewish mourners stirs up deep emotions in Jesus (vv. 33, 35); what is much less clear is what those emotions are. The difficulty in interpreting v. 33 influences the ways in which it is translated. The NRSV describes Jesus with, "he was greatly disturbed in spirit and deeply moved." The NIV describes Jesus with, "he was deeply moved in spirit and troubled." The first verb, *embrimaomai*, occurs only in the Lazarus story in the Fourth Gospel (11:33, 38) and infrequently elsewhere in the New Testament (Mt. 9:30; Mk. 1:43; 14:5). In its non-Johannine

---

[8]For an overview of the critical discussion of the question of priority in the traditions of Martha or Mary, see Rudolf Schnackenburg, *The Gospel According to St. John,* 3 vols. (New York: Seabury, 1982), 2:319–21.

occurrences, the verb is associated neither with mourning nor grief, but occurs in contexts of reproach and rebuke. The second verb used in v. 33, *tarasso,* reinforces this interpretation, because its primary sense is that of disturbance (cf. Jn. 5:7; Acts 15:24; 17:8; Mt. 2:3). Neither of the verbs seems to mean "moved," in the sense of pathos or empathy, as common English language usage would suggest, but something closer to anger. The KJV may be most helpful in its translation of this verse—"he groaned in the spirit, and was troubled"—because it draws attention to the fact that the weeping causes Jesus to be troubled, rather than the more ambiguous "moved."

The difficulty in interpreting Jesus' response here is compounded for the preacher because the image of Jesus weeping in empathy and compassion is so appealing to popular imagination. Yet if we see only empathy, then we lose the chance to explore the harder edge of Jesus' response—that he is troubled, deeply disturbed, perhaps even on the verge of anger. One of the oldest interpretations of Jesus' response here, dating back to the earliest interpreters of the church, still may have the most to offer contemporary interpreters of this verse. John Chrysostom was among the first to suggest that Jesus is angry and distressed because of the evidence of the power of death in the world.[9] The tears of the mourners remind Jesus of how much of the battle with death remains to be fought, that even though he is the light of the world, even though he is the resurrection and the life, death remains a formidable enemy.

Preaching in the face of death is perhaps the most difficult and awesome task in any preacher's ministry. At the time of death, when the bereaved family and friends are at the point of most abject despair, simplistic answers and heartwarming platitudes will not even begin to reach to the core of their despair. Tears and words of empathy are appropriate, but equally important

---

[9]John Chrysostom, Homily 63 on John. John Calvin, in his commentary on John 11:38, also supports this view (see *The Gospel According to St. John 11–21 and The First Epistle of John,* ed. David W. Torrance and Thomas F. Torrance [Grand Rapids, Mich.: Eerdmans, 1959], 13).

is the preacher's willingness to face honestly with the family the devastation that death has wrought in their midst. To rush quickly to affirmations of hope and resurrection without naming the grip that death has on a family is to mock both the power of death and the power of life. If the power of death is minimized, then the power of the resurrection is also minimized, because without a real enemy, the resurrection becomes an empty victory.

Jesus' reactions in vv. 33 and 35 (see also v. 38) show the gospel reader and the preacher that he did not minimize the power of death. He did not greet the evidences of the power of death on those he loved with a quick fix or a reassuring pat. Instead Jesus greeted the evidence of the grip of death with a troubled spirit and groaning tears. He did not simply cry in sympathy, but cried in tumult, because the reality of the power of death has to be confronted. If a preacher can help a family and a congregation face and name the power of death, then real pastoral and theological work has been done and can continue. The church, like much contemporary culture, shies away from thinking and talking about death, as if somehow not talking about it will make death go away. The church talks about victory over death, but does not like to linger over death itself. Jesus' response in these verses suggests that the church does need to linger over death and allow itself as a body to be "greatly disturbed in spirit." Death is an inescapable part of human life, and the church's great gift is not to deny that reality, but to be able to transform that reality through God's gift of life made available in Jesus' triumph over death. The placement of John 11:1–45 on the fifth Sunday of Lent provides an important liturgical moment for preacher and congregation to name the power of death together.

In this moment of tumult and consternation, of facing death head on, Jesus finally turns his attention to Lazarus (v. 34). In v. 11 Jesus told his disciples that he was going to Judea to awaken Lazarus from sleep, yet since his arrival in Bethany, Jesus has been more preoccupied with the two sisters than with the dead-and-buried Lazarus. That Jesus turns toward Lazarus's tomb only after he has faced the reality of death with both sisters and their community may also contain a clue for the preacher who is called to preach in the face of death.

The crowd's response "come and see" (v. 34) echoes the first words of invitation that Jesus spoke to his disciples in the gospel's opening chapter (1:39). This echo may add an additional poignancy to the words, because what the reader first heard as an invitation to new life is now spoken as an invitation to come and see death. Jesus weeps in response to the crowd's invitation (v. 35), and as discussed above, his tears witness to the power of death in the world. Jesus' tears express the pain that death causes in human life.

As in chapter 9, where Jesus' deeds engender a split response, Jesus' weeping engenders a split reaction here. While some interpret Jesus' tears sympathetically, some in the crowd take Jesus' tears as a sign of Jesus' powerlessness in the face of death: "Could not he who opened the eyes of the blind man have kept this man from dying?" The words of this skeptical group make explicit the connection between the healing of John 9 and the Lazarus story, a connection the reader has sensed implicitly since v. 4. The gift of sight and the gift of life both point to the presence of God at work through Jesus.

The Raising of Lazarus (11:38–45)

In v. 38 Jesus finally arrives at the tomb. The church traditionally refers to John 11:1–53 as "the raising of Lazarus," yet the actual raising of Lazarus occupies little time in the telling of the story. Only seven out of forty-four verses of the text take place at the tomb, and the raising of Lazarus is accomplished in two brief verses (vv. 43–44). The Fourth Evangelist has devoted thirty-seven verses to introducing the miracle, in order to establish the appropriate interpretive categories for the reader. In chapter 9, most of the evangelist's interpretive work followed the miracle; here it precedes it. When Jesus arrives at the tomb, greatly disturbed by the power of death (v. 38), the reader knows that the one who stands at the mouth of the tomb is not any common miracle worker. The one who stands at the mouth of the tomb is the resurrection and the life (v. 25a).

Jesus orders the stone to be removed from the cave in which Lazarus is entombed (v. 39). In John 20, when Mary Magdalene arrives at Jesus' tomb, the stone is already removed from the opening. When Mary arrives, the power of death has already been vanquished. At Lazarus's tomb the power of death is still in force. The tomb is still sealed, and Jesus must intercede in order to open the tomb to life.

Martha, absent since v. 28, reappears on the scene and tries to stop Jesus (v. 39). Martha is identified as "the sister of the dead man." Martha is not identified in relation to her living sister, Mary, nor even to Lazarus by name (cf. vv. 5, 28), but is identified only through her relation to a dead man. This detail underscores the centrality of death for the scene that is about to be played out. The power of death can dominate life, even to the point of defining Martha's identity.

In our discussion of vv. 25–27, we noted the distance between Jesus' question and Martha's answer. Jesus asked her if she believed that he was the resurrection and the life, and she answered him with traditional Messianic affirmations. The reader was left with lingering questions—Was Martha's confession adequate? Was her understanding adequate? Martha's protest in v. 39 now answers these questions and confirms the distance between what Jesus offered and what she embraced. She attempts to prevent Jesus from opening the tomb, presenting Jesus with the logical and biological reasons against opening the tomb, much as Nicodemus mustered all kinds of arguments to speak against being born *anothen* (3:4). Jewish burial rites did not include embalming—the body was anointed with perfume and wrapped in burial clothes—so Martha's words about the stench are accurate. No one would be foolish enough to open the tomb of a man four days dead.

Jesus will not be deterred by Martha's protestations. His words to her (v. 40) recall his earlier words of vv. 4, 15, 25–26: "Did

I not tell you that if you believed, you would see the glory of God?" From the opening verses of the chapter (11:4), Jesus has linked Lazarus's death with the glory of God, and Martha's protests at the tomb are a reminder of the difference between what Jesus has seen all along in Lazarus's illness and what the other characters have seen. They have seen only illness (cf. v. 37), but Jesus has recognized an occasion for the revelation of the glory of God. As in Jesus' earlier question to Martha, this question, too, includes the reader in its scope. Both the characters and the reader are directed by Jesus to look with the eyes of faith for the glory of God.

Jesus' words, not Martha's protests, carry the day—the stone is taken away (v. 41a). The anticipated moment for action has come—and once more the Fourth Evangelist works against the reader's expectations. At this most critical and dramatic moment, with the open tomb gaping before the reader, the Fourth Evangelist again slows down the movement of the narrative. Instead of directing his attention to Lazarus's tomb, Jesus lifts his eyes to God and prays. The content of Jesus' prayer is of a piece with his words of v. 41. He has told the gathered crowd that if they believe, they will see the glory of God, and now Jesus thanks God for God's presence with him that enables Jesus to be the revealer of this glory. His words of thanksgiving function like so many of the words in the Lazarus story—to interpret in advance what the characters and reader are about to see. His words express the interconnectedness of his relationship with God that is central to the Fourth Gospel (cf. 3:34–35; 10:30; 12:49; 14:24). God has given Jesus power over life and death (5:21) and the power to raise the dead (5:25–29). This gift from God is central to all Jesus says and does, and this prayer ensures that God's gift is central for the characters and the reader as well.

After forty-two verses of anticipation, the narration of the miracle is terse and lean. After he has prayed, Jesus cries, "Lazarus, come out!" (v. 43). The miracle is accomplished simply by Jesus' voice; the power of Jesus' word awakens Lazarus from the dead. Jesus calls Lazarus by name, just like the good shepherd of John

10 calls his flock by name (10:3). The visual image that the Fourth Evangelist creates in v. 44 is inescapably graphic: "The dead man came out, his hands and feet bound with strips of cloth, and his face wrapped in a cloth." Even though Lazarus is now alive and walking, he is still identified as the "dead man." This description keeps before the reader exactly what Jesus has done, so that there is no escaping the magnitude of Jesus' miracle— he has made a dead man live. It also distinguishes the raising of Lazarus from Jesus' own resurrection. In calling Lazarus the "dead man," the reader is reminded that Lazarus has been resuscitated from death, but he is still defined by his mortality. The risen Jesus will never be identified as the "dead man."

The "dead man" comes out of the tomb still bound in the cloths in which his body had been prepared for burial, and Jesus must give additional commands to free Lazarus from his bindings (v. 44b). These details, too, reinforce the magnitude and nature of Jesus' miracle. Lazarus is still held by the external markers of death, and yet he lives. The detailed description of the condition of Lazarus's body also points ahead to the story of Jesus' death. At Jesus' resurrection, the disposition of the burial cloths is quite different from what happens in the Lazarus story. The Fourth Evangelist devotes two whole verses of chapter 20 (vv. 6–7) to describing the precise location of the linen cloths in the tomb, and the Lazarus story is helpful in understanding why such a detailed description is provided. Unlike Lazarus, Jesus emerges from the tomb unfettered by the bonds of his burial. Lazarus is a dead man who lives again by virtue of the saving words and presence of Jesus. The burial cloths are another reminder of his dependence and mortality. By contrast, Jesus leaves behind all the old signs of death. Not even the clothes of death have any claim on him.

In the Lazarus story, we have a stupendous, world-shattering gift of life. A man, dead, is called out of the tomb and walks out alive. Yet this act in and of itself is not the "point" of the story. This story is not intended to inspire awe in a miracle worker, but to lead to faith in the one who gives life (v. 45) and in the

God who makes this and all gifts possible. The narrative has offered many explicit pointers about how properly to interpret this miracle so that we will not be misled by surface impressions: it is for the glory of God (11:4); that the Son of Man may be glorified through it (v. 4); if you believe, though you die, you will live (v. 25); if you believe, you will see the glory of God (v. 40). All Jesus' words in anticipation of this miracle move the reader to look beyond the stupendous act of reviving the dead to what one can learn and experience about God through that act. As odd as it sounds, the actual raising of Lazarus is narrated as succinctly as it is so that the miracle does not get in the way of the truth of the story. The truth of the story is that Jesus is the resurrection and the life. The Lazarus miracle is one vivid, dramatic embodiment of that truth, but that truth does not depend on the miracle. The truth of Jesus as the resurrection and the life rests on the glory of God that the Lazarus miracle reveals.

Conclusion

As we noted at the beginning of this chapter, John has positioned the Lazarus story in such a way that the gospel reader is impelled to look beyond the upbeat ending of v. 45 to the verses that follow. In the very next verse (v. 46), for example, it becomes clear that not everyone celebrated Jesus' gift of life to Lazarus. Some of the people who witnessed the miracle report it to the Pharisees, and that reporting occasions the meeting at which the formal decision to kill Jesus is made (vv. 47–53). In addition, a decision is also made to kill Lazarus (12:9–11), because Lazarus's presence as a living, breathing man is a constant reminder of the miracle that has occurred.

Is it the preacher's responsibility to bring all those later texts into his or her sermon on John 11:1–45? No, but it is the preacher's responsibility to make sure that he or she preaches nothing that would not stand up to the scrutiny of those subsequent passages. No meaning can be found from John 11:1–45 that is not consonant with the continuation of the

Lazarus story. A celebration of Jesus' gift of life that is not located in the context of Jesus' death is not possible. The Fourth Evangelist has already indicated this to the careful reader and preacher by the number of allusions and references to Jesus' death that are incorporated into the Lazarus story. Jesus' tears and consternation at the power of death also remind the preacher that the gift of life cannot be proclaimed cheaply or easily, as if there is no cost to doing battle with death.

All this makes John 11:1–45 an apt lesson for the end of Lent. The dynamics of this passage reflect the dynamics that the preacher is called to evoke during Lent—lingering over the meaning and significance of a wondrous gift of newness of life that also carries with it the reality of death. Jesus' life is an act of love and grace, and Jesus' death is an act of love and grace, and in the story of the raising of Lazarus the preacher has the chance to contemplate the two together. There is no stronger affirmation of the love and grace of Jesus' life than his raising of Lazarus, and there is no stronger affirmation of the love and grace of his death than the aftermath of the raising of Lazarus. The two are interconnected throughout the Lazarus story, so that if the preacher can only listen to John, he or she may learn something new about the shape of both Jesus' life and death. The good news of Lent and Holy Week, as of the Lazarus story, is that life steps out of an open tomb. When one looks death in the face, one finds the grace of God.

This analysis of John 11 has attempted to demonstrate the importance of how the story is told, not just what the story tells, and to probe the implications of that for preaching. The Fourth Evangelist does not merely *tell* the reader that "the Son gives life to whomever he wishes" (5:21), but *shows* the reader what it means to speak of Jesus as the one who gives life. Jesus' power over death is not restricted to 11:43–44, but is present throughout the narrative as Jesus breaks open the death-dealing categories according to which the disciples, Mary and Martha, and the Jews attempt to live. In this text, the Fourth Evangelist has created a narrative world in which the reader can experience Jesus as the resurrection and the life. The preacher is called to recreate that world for the congregation.

The greatest wonder of this story may be that despite Mary and Martha's inability to understand what Jesus is about and to grasp fully what he has to offer, Jesus offers life anyway. To those who are open, to those who grieve, to those who will risk the experience of being transformed by Jesus, Jesus offers life. "Lazarus, come out," he says, and out walks a man known to be dead, four days in the tomb. The dead man lives. The old order no longer reigns. We see the glory of God.

Sermons

Food and Work

(John 6:24–41)

**Propers 12, 13, and 14, Year B
Thanksgiving Day, Year C**

Food and work. Two such simple words, two words that form such an integral part of our daily existence. At the most basic level in an urban culture, we eat so that we have energy for work; we work so that we have money enough for food. These two simple words lie at the heart of this rather intricate text from the gospel of John. Yet as we live into this text, we discover that the meaning of both food and work turns out to be quite different from what one might first assume.

To the crowd, food means an amazing meal of bread and fish. Just the day before they had eaten bread and fish that Jesus had blessed and distributed to them, and now they wondered where he was, where he had gone to. The feeding of the more than five thousand men, women, and children had, I imagine, been a hot topic of conversation all night—how much bread did you get? Did you get any fish? Did he put the bread right in your hand? It probably was a bit disappointing to return to the site of this wondrous feeding and discover that Jesus and the disciples were gone. And so, the people get into their boats and cross the Sea of Galilee to find Jesus.

To Jesus, food means something quite different—and he puts that difference to the crowd as soon as it finds him: "Very truly, I tell you, you are looking for me, not because you saw signs, but because you ate your fill of the loaves." Jesus knows that the crowd is seeking him not because of what they saw of God in the feeding, but because, quite simply, they ate their fill. And

Jesus knows something else that the crowd has yet to learn: the food from the day before, that morsel of bread, that piece of fish, sure it was good, sure it filled you up, but it's gone, isn't it? And you can keep eating and eating and eating, but you will not be satisfied. And so Jesus tells the crowd, "Do not work for the food that perishes, but for the food that endures for eternal life, which the Son of Man will give you."

Now, I spend a lot of time in the gospel of John and I know how these conversations with Jesus usually turn out, so if I were the crowd, I would quit while I was ahead, get back in my boat, and go home. But no—they think they understand Jesus, and so they say, "Okay, well, if you want to talk about work instead of food, we can do that—what must we do to work the works of God?" Jesus speaks of work as a gift, as receiving from the Son of Man the food that endures to eternal life. The crowd speaks of work as works, things at which they must labor. They think that they must do the works of God; they have not yet seen that the works of God are manifest in Jesus and do not depend at all on their labors. Jesus offers them grace, the promise of food that will not perish, of sustenance that will never end, but that grace vanishes in the crowd's response. Their question about their own works assumes a self-sufficiency that blocks their ability to receive a gift of grace. Jesus and the crowd speak with the same vocabulary, but they do not speak the same language.

So Jesus tries again: "This is the work of God, that you believe in him whom God has sent." "Work," it seems, is not *doing* anything; "work" is simply *being*—living in and out of faith. "Work" is our response to God's work in Jesus; "work" is our relationship to God and Jesus in faith. Jesus keeps trying to speak to the crowd in the cadences of grace—work is defined not by what we do, but by who and what God has sent.

And once again the crowd deflects the language of grace, turning the language of gift into the language of contingency and demand, "What sign are you going to give us then, so that we may see it and believe you? What work are you performing? Our ancestors ate the manna in the wilderness." Now remember, this is the same crowd who ate bread and fish with Jesus on the other side of the Sea of Galilee. How can they ask Jesus to do a work? Are they suffering from extreme short-term memory loss? No, they are suffering the effects of thinking that the food they ate was only intended to fill them up. If their self-sufficiency blocked Jesus' first words of grace, their consumption blocks the renewed offer of grace here. They consumed the bread and fish gladly—but it is gone and they need more food. There is no gift, no sign pointing to the presence of God, because the gift and the presence are consumed in our appetite for consumption.

Still undaunted, Jesus speaks the cadences of grace one more time. He names for them where God was in the feeding and also names explicitly the gift: "For the bread of God is that which comes down from heaven and gives life to the world." And the crowd, eager for the best bread, says, "Give us this bread always." But this bread cannot be given like that. The bread of God is not about consuming; it is not about satiation; it is the gift of life. It is not something to be demanded, but something to be received. It cannot be *given always,* because that is not how this bread satisfies our appetites. This bread is present and available *always,* because it is given *once,* in the very person and life of Jesus, the incarnate presence of God's grace.

"I am the bread of life. Whoever comes to me will never be hungry, and whoever believes in me will never be thirsty." This, then, is our work; this is our food—to live into the life of the one who loves us, to live into the promises of the one who gives us life. What we need for life is available in Jesus—his grace sustains us and so takes away our drive for self-sufficiency; his gift of love feeds us and so sates our appetites. Our labor is redefined. We no longer have to work our way into some kind of security, because we are already safe—Jesus will not drive us away nor lose anything of all that God has given him. Our present and our future rest in God's and Jesus' hands; we only have to enter and embrace them.

This text invites us to see that food and work are neither what we consume nor what we do. They are instead the promises we receive and out of which we live. The work of faith, of the faithful, is to allow ourselves to be fed by Jesus. The work of faith is not easy work, because it goes against our understanding of what it means to work, achieve, and accomplish. This understanding is at the heart of the American dream that if we only work hard enough, we will then have all good things. And while all good things most often take the form of bigger and better possessions, that is not the only form that our acquisitive sense of food and work takes. We also seem to think that if we go to enough church activities, schedule enough meetings, teach one more Sunday school class, we will then also have all good things from God.

It is hard to accept that our true work is to trust, to believe in the life-giving promises of God. But try as we might, we can never work hard enough—at home, on the job, in our communities—to create these promises ourselves. We can never be good enough, industrious enough, virtuous enough to assuage our hunger and thirst, because the end of hunger and thirst comes only when we fall back in faith on the sustaining promises of God.

"I am the bread of life. Whoever comes to me will never be hungry, and whoever believes in me will never be thirsty." Our hunger and thirst will never be assuaged if we insist on holding to our self-sufficiency in our work, on our ability to work ourselves into new life as if we are the authors of God's works and promises. When we work so hard at working, we will miss the offer of grace. If we cling to our own definitions of food that fills and work that consumes, we will inevitably deflect the words of life.

But thanks be to God, when we remember that work is being with God in faith, we will truly taste the bread of life, and we will never be hungry or thirsty. Our life-giving work is to receive the gifts and grace of God in Jesus, and those gifts will never disappoint.

"My Sheep Hear My Voice"

(Psalm 23; Revelation 7:9–17; John 10:22–30)

Fourth Sunday of Easter, Year C

In the gospel lesson, the religious authorities come up to Jesus in the temple—well into his ministry, after he has healed an invalid, given sight to the blind, turned water into wine, fed multitudes from five loaves and two fish, preached the possibilities of new life grounded in God's love over and over again—and ask him, "How long will you keep us in suspense? If you are the Messiah, tell us plainly."

And Jesus, exercising considerable self-restraint, says, "I told you, and you do not believe; I showed you, and you do not see." And then—as if this should settle it— "You do not believe, because you do not belong to my sheep."

That's the answer? "You do not belong to my sheep?" How about: You do not believe, because your doctrine is not right? Or—you do not believe, because you are fallen and depraved? Or—you do not believe, because you do not work hard enough? No, only this—you do not belong to my sheep.

Then, with great gentleness, Jesus paints a picture of what it means to be his sheep: "My sheep hear my voice. I know them, and they follow me. I give them eternal life, and they will never perish. No one will snatch them out of my hand." To be Jesus' sheep is to be led to life, safe, sheltered in the palm of his hand. To be Jesus' sheep is to be known by him and to follow where he leads. To be Jesus' sheep is to trust the sound of his voice, to trust the voice of God that speaks through Jesus' words. Because it is the safety of God's hand that assures the safety of Jesus' hand; it is God we see and trust in Jesus. "The Father and I are one."

The world, it seems, then, consists not of sheep and goats (apologies to Matthew) but of sheep and those who are not sheep. And all of us—students foremost, but also faculty and staff— are at seminary to learn to be sheep. You came to seminary to learn to listen to and for the shepherd's voice, to follow where the shepherd leads, to receive the gifts the shepherd prepares. And if, as you move through seminary and out into the church, you forget that you are sheep, the game is lost. If you remember you are sheep, surely goodness and mercy will follow you all the days of your life.

How can you forget that you are sheep? Easy—by thinking instead that you are shepherds. Let's look again at the religious authorities who question Jesus in the temple. John calls these authorities "the Jews," but it is important for us to remember that he does not mean the Jewish people. John uses the expression "the Jews" to refer to those leaders and authorities within Jesus' own religious tradition who resisted him, who would not allow the newness he offered to penetrate the systems and structures they had taken generations to construct. For contemporary Christians, Jesus' own people are Christians, not Jews, and therefore, those authorities and powers who resist the voice of Jesus need to be sought within the church, not outside it. For "the Jews" in this gospel lesson, then, we need to think of those among Jesus' "own" who hold tightly to power and control, religious authorities in the church who know how all questions should be posed and what answers are acceptable, how things are done, where God is found. We need to think of "Christians" who are so intent on being shepherds themselves that they no longer listen as sheep for the voice of Jesus.

The religious authorities in the gospel lesson think they are in charge ("How long will you keep us in suspense? Tell us plainly." In other words, do it our way) and hence cannot be sheep. Those who hold to power cannot/will not/must not listen to the voice of Jesus, who challenges their tightly constructed

world, because to listen to the voice of Jesus means that they
are only sheep, never shepherds. And those in charge have spent
so much, given so much to be shepherds; how could they face
being mere sheep again? Yet that is the choice Jesus puts before
them, before us: be sheep, not shepherds; let God and me be
the shepherd.

Jesus' words about sheep echo the psalm appointed for the
day, Psalm 23. Who would resist being a sheep if one could be
tended by such a shepherd?

> The LORD is my shepherd, I shall not want.
> He makes me lie down in green pastures;
> He leads me beside still waters;
>> he restores my soul.
> He leads me in right paths for his name's sake.

In singing about God the shepherd, the psalmist tries so hard
to be objective, to report on what the shepherd does in third-
person language—the Lord does this and the Lord does that.
But the gracious gifts of the good shepherd ultimately overpower
his song, and the psalmist must address God directly: You are
with me; you prepare a table for me; you anoint my head with
oil. I am your sheep, sings the psalmist. Though I walk through
life's darkest moments, I am not afraid of any evil, because I know
you watch over me with your shepherd's rod and staff. Psalm
23 paints an irresistible picture of what it means to live as God's
sheep, to let God be the shepherd.

The shepherd's care is offered in the midst of conflict and
fear: the presence of my enemies, the darkest valley, hunger, thirst,
homelessness, abandonment. The shepherd's care is intimate,
elemental, immediate. It sounds forth in the day's other lesson,
"They will hunger no more, and thirst no more; the sun will
not strike them, nor any scorching heat; for the Lamb at the
center of the throne will be their shepherd, and he will guide
them to springs of the water of life, and God will wipe away
every tear from their eyes" (Rev. 7:16–17). It is such basic,
primal imagery to evoke the shepherd's care, because what does

one need and long for most when one is crying but to have one's tears wiped away by a loving hand?

What the psalmist celebrates, what the author of Revelation promises, what Jesus in John describes as the shape of the life of faith—this is what it means to be a sheep. To trust one's life to God's tender, watchful care. To place one's fears and needs in God's sheltering hand. To live out one's days in the sure attention of Jesus' protecting hand. To listen. To follow. And like the psalmist and the great hymnist of Revelation, to give thanks to the shepherd.

Does this mean, then, that you are at seminary spending time and all this money, asking so much of those who love you, so that you can end up where you started: as God's sheep? Well—yes and no. Yes, because there can be no more grace-filled life than to be a sheep in God's flock. And no, because the time you spend at seminary teaches you—us—to be sheep in ways that were not possible and available before. We learn to hear and recognize the voice of the shepherd in the complex and conflicted pages of scripture, in the great cloud of witnesses—some noble, some ignoble –who people the history of the church. We learn to ask questions about theology and ethics that will help us to see what is at stake when one follows the shepherd. We learn to recognize the face of the shepherd in the faces of the poor and the despised, to hear the anguished voice of the shepherd in the pain-filled voices of the rejected, the lonely, the helpless, the forlorn.

God willing, in your time here you will learn to listen to the world's pain, your pain, the church's pain. You will know how and for what to cry, and why the shepherd's hand is needed to wipe away tears. You will know where food is needed, where thirst is real, and what a miracle it is when, in the face of all that, it is still possible to envision still waters, overflowing cups, green pastures.

Yes, sisters and brothers in Christ, we are learning much, but if we begin to think that knowing these things positions us as the shepherd, instead of sheep, think again. "My sheep hear my voice. I know them, and they follow me." This is the life of ministry, this is the life of faith: to share with all God's sheep in the restorative, grace-filled gifts of God.

The Fragrance of Love

(John 12:1–8)

Fifth Sunday of Lent, Year C

Although John does not tell us explicitly why this dinner party is given for Jesus, it is easy to make an educated guess. Not too many days before, this same group of friends had been assembled at a tomb and had watched and listened while Jesus called Lazarus out of the tomb, called Lazarus out of death and back into life. This same group of friends were the ones to whom Jesus said, "Unbind him and let him go," and so they removed the bonds of death and received Lazarus back into human fellowship. And this is also the same group of friends who had tried initially to stop Jesus from opening the tomb, because as Martha put it so unambiguously, "Lord, already there is a stench because he has been dead four days." What they trusted and feared, this group of friends, was the stench of death—a stench more powerful and pervasive than any man standing at the mouth of the tomb. It was a stench designed to keep away the living and to announce, through its putrid wafting, that death had won, that death was the only end of the story. But Jesus was not afraid of the stench of death, and in front of this group of friends, he called Lazarus into life.

And so, here they are again, this same group of friends, with Lazarus in their company. This dinner party, in fact, seems to be the first time they have all been assembled since that day at the tomb—because Jesus left Bethany immediately after that day. For you see, not everyone was pleased with Jesus' conquest over the stench of death. The religious authorities in Jerusalem saw the raising of Lazarus for what it was—putting the world on notice that God's power for life was stronger than death—and knew that there was no stopping this Jesus, unless they stopped him permanently. So, as the immediate aftermath of that day at the tomb, the religious authorities issued an arrest warrant for Jesus and put him under a formal death sentence.

Two events, then, draw this group of friends to the table in Bethany, a Jerusalem suburb, six days before Passover—joy and thanksgiving for Lazarus's return to life, and the reality of the threat that closes in on Jesus. Even at this table, where life is being celebrated and renewed, a new stench of death pervades the scene.

And it is the same with us in Lent—drawn together, indeed, today drawn together at the table, to celebrate and affirm God's power for life, and yet we know also that the stench of death is with us too. It is with us, not only because to move from today to Easter we will have to walk with Jesus through the valley of death—but also because each way we turn, even in this most beautiful of springs, we know that death sits waiting. The death of a family member, the sudden illness of a valued friend, a senseless act of violence, refugees on the road again, words of hate and greed, homeless children, loveless families—it is there, everywhere, the stench of death. Why bother to roll away the stone? It has been much more than four days, and already there is a stench.

And yet in the face of this cosmic struggle between life and death, in the face of the very stench of death that threatens to claim all of God's goodness and life, at this table in Bethany, a strange and wondrous act occurs. An act that puts death on notice that it can come, but we will not accept the terms of its coming.

Martha has served the food, and it is again easy to imagine the conversation as dishes are passed around the table: "Do you remember how Lazarus looked when he came out of the tomb?" "Hey, Lazarus—take a bath yet?" "Do you believe that Jesus just said, 'Come out'—and there Lazarus was?" "But what will happen next? You know, the authorities want to arrest him?" "Are you afraid?"

And then—conversation stops for a moment, and all eyes turn to Mary. For she takes a pound of the most expensive perfume, pours it over Jesus' feet, and then wipes Jesus' feet with her hair. Conversation resumes immediately, initiated by Judas, who protests the waste of money. It is amazing to me how many people seem to take Judas's words as an accurate assessment of this scene, as if the anointing really is about money and proper stewardship. John repeatedly shows us how untrustworthy Judas's words are—he is the betrayer; he is a thief. Don't follow Judas as a guide through this story, because Judas is the partner of death.

Instead—follow Mary. Let's look again at what Mary does. She anoints Jesus' feet and wipes Jesus' feet with her hair. Anoints his feet, wipes his feet. Why anoint his feet with perfume, if she is immediately going to wipe them dry? To many commentators, Mary's actions seem merely an awkward echo of the story of the woman who anoints Jesus' feet in Luke 7; they note that the woman's action of wiping her tears from Jesus' feet with her hair fits the Lukan story, but such a gesture seems out of place in the Johannine account.

Careful attention to the Fourth Evangelist's word choice in narrating Mary's actions, however, suggests that the action of wiping Jesus' feet is essential to the Johannine story. The verb "wipe" is the same verb used to describe Jesus' wiping of his disciples' feet at the foot washing in John 13:5. Mary's anointing and wiping of Jesus' feet thus points toward Jesus' footwashing at the Last Supper. Jesus will wash his disciples' feet as an expression of his love for them, as a way of drawing them into his life with God. He will ask them to love one another as he has loved them. What Jesus will do for his disciples and will ask them to do for one another, Mary has already done for him here. Her act shows forth the love that will be the hallmark of discipleship in John.

The power of the witness of Mary's act of love here is that she knows how to respond to Jesus without being told. She fulfills

Jesus' love commandment before he even teaches it; she embraces Jesus' death before he has even taught his followers about its true meaning. In the anointing, she shows what it means to be one of Jesus' own. She gives boldly and extravagantly of herself in love to Jesus, just as Jesus will give boldly and extravagantly of himself in love at his death.

Jesus knows this about Mary's act. Note how he rebuffs Judas and embraces Mary's actions. In this anointing, which does indeed also foreshadow the anointing of a body for burial, Mary has acknowledged the presence of the stench of death. She does not flinch from it; she looks Jesus' death straight in the eye—but she will not be cowed. She is not cowed, because her love for Jesus, her love for the love and life that he embodies, emboldens her not only to be unafraid of death, but in fact to taunt it.

Listen again to this one verse, a little detail I have so far skipped over in the reimagining of this dinner party, because I have wanted to save the best for last. "The house was filled with the fragrance of the perfume." Think about it for a minute, or better, sniff/ inhale it for a minute. Mary anointed Jesus' feet with a pound of perfume. Sixteen ounces of perfume, of the costly perfume, pure nard, intensely fragrant. Sixteen ounces of perfume poured over Jesus' feet and then wiped into Mary's hair. I occasionally wear a drop or two of rose perfume (not the costliest!), and it always astounds me how many people will say "Rose? That's nice," from one tiny drop. Sixteen ounces—of course the whole house smelled. Perfume overkill, don't you think?

Yes, perfume overkill I do think. Because that's it, you see— perfume overkill. The fragrance of love. At Lazarus's tomb, Mary's sister attempted to stop Jesus because of the stench of death. And now, through Mary's act, the stench of death that once lingered over this household and haunts the edges of this meal has been replaced by the fragrance of love and devotion.

That is how we meet and defeat the stench of death—we overwhelm it with the fragrance of love for Jesus and one another. We love so boldly and extravagantly that the whole house is filled with the fragrance of the perfume. Will death come? Yes. It will come for Jesus; it will come to those we love; it will come to us. But its stench will not overwhelm us. We will love as Jesus loved us—and perhaps, just perhaps, the world will be filled with the fragrance of his perfume.

"To Have a Share with Jesus"

(John 13:1–20)

Holy Thursday, Years A, B, and C

For all the formality of the language with which this story from John begins, the setting is really very simple. It is a dinner party gathering of friends that takes place right before a big holiday. A table laden with food and drink, people talking—some shouting loudly across the room, some whispering quietly to the person sitting or standing next to them. If the evening is going well, the guests are aware of none of the background work and preparation for the meal; they are only aware of their immediate experience of good food and good company. The host or hostess, by contrast, is attuned to every detail of setting and preparation, to every detail that makes the meal a hospitable occasion for the guests.

The evening meal narrated in John 13 is no exception to this rhythm of host and guest—except that at this party, the host is not preoccupied with how the food and drink are holding up (that seems to have been his mother's job at an earlier party), but is acutely attuned to the occasion that the dinner marks. An occasion of which as yet, his dinner guests are singularly unaware.

Indeed, the gospel storyteller is at great pains to tell us all the things that are going on inside Jesus' mind as this dinner unfolds: "Jesus knew that his hour had come to depart from this world and go to the Father;" "Jesus, knowing that the Father had given all things into his hands, and that he had come from God and was going to God." For Jesus to know that his hour has come means that Jesus knows that the end of his life is upon him. The arrival of Jesus' hour marks the end of Jesus' ministry in "this world": he will no longer be a physical, bodily presence to his disciples and in the world. His incarnate ministry and mission in the world is coming to an end. It is this knowledge that Jesus carries with him into the dinner party. And he also carries with him a knowledge of the shape and source of his ministry and identity—everything that he has and does and everything that he is can be traced to his origins with God. It is as one fully in union with God, the giver of all gifts, that Jesus hosts this meal. And when the events of the hour play themselves out in Jesus' death, resurrection, and ascension, Jesus will return to this giving God.

This is a lot to know as one hosts a dinner party! But the writer of the gospel of John lets us see one other detail to which Jesus attends as he hosts this meal, and this detail gives Jesus' knowledge its defining shape: "having loved his own who were in the world, he loved them to the end." The Greek expression translated by the NRSV as "to the end" is a marvelously ambiguous expression. It can function as an adverb of time and thus mean "he loved them to the very last moment," appropriate in this context of Jesus' hour. Or it can function to describe how one loves; thus Jesus loves "totally, completely," or as the NIV translates it, "the full extent of his love." We probably are to understand both meanings here, because what the gospel storyteller wants to impress upon us is the limitlessness of Jesus' love. There is nothing that limits Jesus' love for his own, nothing that marks the boundaries of that love. It is a love whose essence is its unfathomable fullness.

This, then, is what the host of this dinner brings to his party— knowledge of his own imminent death, knowledge of his relationship with God, and the lived experience of love without limits. His guests eat, drink, and converse, unaware of the full extent of the host's preparation that makes this gathering possible.

So let's imagine ourselves at this party again, a plate in one hand, glass in another, mouth full of food, head full of a million fragments of conversation. When our host enters the room, we smile at him to indicate our appreciation and enjoyment of his hospitality—but instead of checking to see if any of the food dishes need to be replenished, he takes off his suit jacket, ties a towel around his waist, pours water into a basin, and calls us over one by one to wash our feet. Hello??? What exactly is going on here? It is the middle of the party. We are quite comfortably ensconced, and the host wants to wash our feet? To put Peter's words in a more contemporary idiom, "I'm outta here."

Now to be honest, foot washing would not seem as strange to a dinner guest in the first century Mediterranean world as it would to a dinner guest in twenty-first century Atlanta. In both Jewish and Greco-Roman settings, foot washing was a way of welcoming one's guests into one's home. A traveler's feet would become dusty during the journey, and the host offered water so that guests could wash their feet. So foot washing as a gesture of hospitality would be recognized as an accepted social practice, but foot washing by the host himself in the *middle* of the dinner party? I don't think so! Foot washing usually was offered as guests arrived and before food was served, not when the party was in full swing. The foot washing was normally performed either by the guests themselves or by servants at the behest of the host. Even first-century guests would be scratching their heads! What kind of gesture is this? What kind of host is this?

Peter seems pretty certain that he knows what kind of gesture it is, and he does not like it one bit. He will not have his lord and teacher, the host of this supper, doing the work of the hired help. He tells Jesus in no uncertain terms that Jesus will never wash his feet. And in response, Jesus says the words on which the whole foot washing narrative depends: "Unless I wash you, you have no share with me." What an odd expression! How can having one's feet washed by Jesus give one a share with him?

To understand Jesus' words and his action, we have to stop thinking about this story from the perspective of the party guests, and return to the perspective of the host. It is Jesus' knowledge and love that lead him to wash his disciples' feet, and it is this knowledge and love to which he gives expression in this deceptively simple gesture of hospitality. In washing his disciples' feet, Jesus says to his disciples, "My house is your house; what is mine is yours." And since Jesus' ultimate home is with God, and what Jesus has to give is a love that knows no limits, in this gesture of hospitality Jesus welcomes the disciples into the circle of love that marks his and God's relationship to each other and to the world. Now such a love and such a relationship is not without cost, for the love that leads Jesus to lay down his outer garment and wash his disciples' feet will also lead him to lay down his life. And the foot washing gives the disciples a share in the whole story, not just part. To have Jesus wash one's feet is to receive from Jesus an act of graciousness and hospitality that decisively alters one's relationship to Jesus, and through Jesus, to God. It is to accept the host's welcome into his home.

No wonder Peter reconsiders his initial reaction to Jesus' gesture and now says, "not my feet only but also my hands and my head!" And perhaps also no wonder that three times in this story of the foot washing we are reminded of Judas's act of betrayal, because such a radical and all-encompassing gesture of love can be difficult to embrace. It is important to remember that Judas did not stand outside the circle of those whose feet Jesus washed this evening, but rather inside it, breaking bread with him, sharing in the host's hospitality. To have a share with Jesus through the foot washing must mean more than to have one's feet washed and toweled dry by Jesus. Judas had done that. In order to have one's share with Jesus, one must choose to accept and be embraced by the gesture of love that Jesus makes in the foot washing. And if one rejects this offer of love for fear of the cost, then one removes oneself from Jesus and the promises of God that are embodied in him.

What an odd turn of events—a dinner party becomes the occasion to have one's life re-formed through the love of God in Jesus. The dinner guest is no longer the somewhat passive recipient of the host's generosity and hospitality, but is called to receive a gift of love that will forever alter how he or she lives in the world. To accept the share with Jesus that is offered through his act of love in the foot washing is to take on a new identity that is shaped and determined by Jesus' hospitality and love. It is to live in the world as one whose feet have been washed by Jesus, as one who has been loved to the limit, as one who has been included in the simplest and yet most profound offer of grace and generosity.

Yet the church often misses this dimension of hospitality and generosity in its appropriation of the foot washing story. The church most often tells this story so that all the emphasis falls on Jesus' words about service near the end of the story. The foot washing scene is appealed to as an example of the need for humble and selfless service, a service in which we often take some pride. But the heart of this story is not some general call to service; the heart of this story is Jesus' love-filled hospitality. If we are to heed Jesus' words and do what Jesus has done, then we need to begin *first* by receiving the gift Jesus offers in the foot washing, *then* embodying the love that he has offered us. This is a story that should point us toward Jesus and his work, not toward ourselves. The church tends to turn the foot washing into a story of the roles we can play as servant, and forget that it is first a story about our willingness to place ourselves quite literally in Jesus' hands. Service for the sake of service, service that is more consumed by doing than by being, is not the example of service that Jesus enacts in the foot washing. Service that makes visible the love and hospitality with God that foot washing makes visible—that is the example Jesus sets for us.

To have the share with Jesus promised in this story is to assume a new identity as a people of God, an identity shaped by the one whose generosity and hospitality knows no bounds. Whether he washes our feet or feeds us bread and wine, it is his hospitality that gives us life and holds the sure promise of love for the world.

"Protect Them in Your Name"

(John 17:6–19)

Seventh Sunday of Easter, Year B

Our society is suffused with prayer. Not only are church people admonished to pray all the time, but in the broader culture, prayer also is everywhere. City councils have prayer breakfasts; we watch basketball players cross themselves and pray before taking a foul shot. Yet in the midst of all this praying, many questions about prayer persist, more questions than we usually allow ourselves to ask. Do we know how to pray, to whom to pray, who we are when we pray? Do we know God is there? Do we hold God to anything when we pray? Do we hope anything, do we imagine anything, do we dare anything when we pray?

In prayer we have the chance to open our lives to the fullness of God's hopes and promises and care. Such openness can be painful, because of the gap between what is promised and what is. There are so many places where God's promises are but a glimmer in the night, and it is often easier to give in to the despair of how things are than to believe that God offers another way. Our prayer time is a time to remember and rejoice that God has promised another way, a better way. Our prayer is the chance to hope enough, imagine enough, and dare enough to know that even in the midst of turmoil and distress, God is present, waiting to bring us home. We are called to be bold enough to trust God's promises and address God in prayer.

Jesus also had to hope enough, to imagine enough, to dare enough to address God in prayer. Our gospel text this morning is Jesus' prayer—or a piece of Jesus' prayer—to his God. And the most amazing thing about this prayer, the part of this prayer that should give us most pause, is that Jesus hopes enough, imagines enough, dares enough to address God in prayer about his followers, about those who believe in him. He does not pray for himself. He does not pray in broad generalizations for the world. In this prayer, this intimate piece of communication between Jesus and his Father, Jesus prays for us.

This prayer from the gospel of John takes place at the end of the Farewell Discourse in John—after the foot washing and before the passion story. Jesus is about to die, and he knows it; he talks to his disciples sometimes as if his crucifixion has already taken place. Jesus is about to die, and with all that in front of him, with all that just hours ahead of him, Jesus pauses, lifts his eyes toward heaven, and prays to God for his followers. He is about to die, and he pauses to speak to God on our behalf.

It is an odd contradiction for us, here in the Easter season. We have moved through trial and crucifixion and have celebrated the triumph of the resurrection, so that as a church we feel ready to imagine the hopes and dreams that Easter makes possible. But in this gospel lesson, Jesus has not yet moved through trial and crucifixion, he has not yet risen from the tomb. Instead, Jesus stands at the very crossroads that leads to his death, and in the face of death, Jesus nonetheless prays the hope of the Easter promise.

What makes such hope possible? Jesus is able to pray to God in confidence, even at the most extreme moment of his life, because of the confidence that has governed his entire life—that God is fully with him. It is confidence in this always abiding divine presence into which Jesus has invited his disciples in his words at this last gathering—and which he now enacts for them in this prayer.

What does Jesus hope for his followers? What does Jesus pray for his followers? The text of John 17:11–19 contains many words and repetitive phrases, but at its heart, we hear these hopes for Jesus' followers: That even when Jesus is absent, God will keep them in God's name, the name they have come to know through

Jesus. That through that name they may be one, even as God and Jesus are one. That Jesus' joy may be completed in them. Jesus has worked hard among his followers and for his followers: he has guarded them, he has given them God's word, and now he prays that in his absence God will continue to be present for the disciples. Jesus prays that in the specificity of daily lives, God will keep his followers from evil; that in the cosmic battle between good and evil that is waging all around, his followers will not succumb to the wrong side. And finally, Jesus prays that God will sanctify his followers in truth—allow the full experience of God's presence in Jesus to direct all their days.

Such wondrous things Jesus prays for those who follow him! I do not think that in our wildest imaginings we could come up with such empowering hopes for ourselves—but Jesus can. Jesus prays for our lives in ways that defy imagination, in ways that are more daring than we can ever hope to pray. Jesus prays for us, and when we listen to Jesus' prayer, our sense of our identity is changed. Jesus is about to die, and he prays for us, that our lives in his absence will be full of God, that together his followers will be God's people in a hostile and uncomprehending world.

The picture of life lived in fulfillment of this prayer is not an easy one. Just as Jesus met resistance and opposition, those who follow Jesus will also be questioned and challenged. If Jesus' followers truly embrace the vision that Jesus prays for them here, then the world will hate them, because the conventional practices of greed, hostility, injustice, and oppression are constantly called into question by the church's witness in the world. This prayer celebrates that Jesus' followers have been sent into a hating and hostile world equipped only with Jesus' prayer for them to God.

What kind of equipping is that? Is this all that Jesus could think of to prepare us—a prayer? Here we are, after Easter, Jesus has ascended to God, just as he said he would, and what are we to do? How are we to live as an Easter people in the days after the resurrection? There are no instructions in this text, no guidelines or directions in this prayer. How will we know evil? How will we know the truth? How can we be sure that God will keep Jesus' followers in God's name?

What kind of gospel lesson is this anyway? With all these questions in front of me, I want to push at this text until I can make it say something else—something more helpful, something more usable, something more practical. I want to reach inside the text and grab Jesus and shake him and say, "Jesus, you can't do this to us. You are leaving us. You are going to leave us alone. You've told us that time after time. Don't just stand there and talk to God. Talk to us. Tell us something relevant and specific that we can do in a hostile and uncomprehending world."

But this text does not budge. And Jesus does not budge. Jesus does not talk to us. Jesus talks only to God. In prayer. That is the mystery of this text and the good news of this gospel lesson: Jesus does not talk directly to us here; Jesus talks to God for us. If these words had been spoken to us, I can guarantee that we would mess them up somehow. If Jesus had turned to his followers instead of to God at the end of the Last Supper and said, "All right, Peter and company, I want you all to be one; I want you all to stay away from evil; I want you all to keep yourselves in God's name"—if Jesus had said these things to his followers, sooner rather than later, each generation of believers would have discovered that it isn't that easy to be one, that it isn't that easy to stay away from the evil one, that it isn't that easy to stay in God's name. We would discover that we were destined to fail, unable to do the tasks Jesus assigned us, unable to follow Jesus' instruction. And we would be alone again, staring at each other blankly around the supper table, having no resources to be in the world but not of the world.

That is why Jesus knew better than to leave things to us. Jesus knew better than to trust us to take care of things ourselves. Jesus knew that there was only one way for us not to be alone when he left, only one way for us to have resources to be in but not of the world—and so Jesus was bold enough to pray to God for us. We do not go alone into a hating and uncomprehending world, because Jesus hoped enough, imagined enough, dared enough to pray for us. In this text, Jesus reminds God of what God has promised and hoped for those into whose midst God has sent Jesus—and he holds God to those promises.

Jesus knows our failings. He knows that if he entrusted our lives and our mission to us alone, we would turn both to our own advantage—and neither our lives nor God's mission would be served. He knows that if he entrusted our lives and our mission to us alone, to our human resources, that our lives and our mission would run dry very soon. Thankfully, Jesus had the imagination, Jesus had the confidence, Jesus had the grace to entrust our lives and our mission to God. Jesus prays for us, and because he prays for us, we can live. Jesus prays for us, and because he prays for us, we can serve. Jesus prays for us. Jesus is bold enough to envision a life for us in which God is fully present—and to entrust the keeping of that vision, the nurture of that vision, to God and God alone.

This prayer in the gospel of John is a powerful demonstration of the love that God and Jesus have for us. Jesus prays for us, entrusts us to God's loving kindness, and somehow we are no longer alone. We are no longer alone in a world that frightens us, perplexes us, tempts us to despair. We can face into the disease of our personal lives, the injustices of a world that so often seems to have gone mad, because we have this text to remind us that our lives are held in God's loving, watchful care. We can act with freedom and confidence, in the face of all odds, because we abide with God, and as the epistle reminds us, "God is love, and those who abide in love abide in God, and God abides in them" (1 Jn. 4:16). God loves us: of that this prayer leaves no doubt, and so we are free to act out that love.

In this prayer Jesus boldly, hopefully, confidently entrusts our lives to God. May Jesus' boldness, hope, and confidence be ours, so that we may live each day in God's watchful presence, empowered by that presence to live into God's promises and Jesus' hopes for us. As Jesus prayed for us, so may we live. Amen.

From Fear to Joy

(John 20:19–23)

Day of Pentecost, Year A
[Second Sunday of Easter, Years A, B, and C]

Today we celebrate Pentecost, the day the church was born through the gift of the Holy Spirit. The story of Pentecost with which we are most familiar is the story from Acts 2—the rush of a mighty wind, tongues of fire, ecstatic, exuberant utterances in many languages. Pentecost in Acts is bold, dramatic, and very public—the gift of the Holy Spirit writ large enough for the whole world to see and take note. There is another Pentecost story, however, another narrative of the day the church received the Holy Spirit. The gospel lesson from John does not shout out to us the way the Acts story does, but instead gently, softly beckons us onward—to watch and listen and wait with the first disciples.

John's story is set on the evening of Easter day, but we do not find ourselves among a jubilant, triumphant gathering of disciples. We have instead the community at its most confused, most dispirited, standing at the brink of defeat and despair. Yes, some of their number had seen the empty tomb, had seen the stone rolled away from the opening, had seen the linen cloths in which the body had been wrapped. And yes, Mary had said to them, "I have seen the Lord," and she had told them all that the risen Jesus had said to her. But who dared to believe Mary's words or to trust what their own eyes had seen at the tomb? After all, they had also seen his limp, dead body removed from the cross, had seen him lain in the tomb, had seen the stone rolled in front to seal the tomb shut. They too had seen the Lord—dead—and how could the work of death be undone?

147

And so it was that they gathered together that night: sorrowful and afraid and confused. Jesus had promised them so many things—his peace, his presence, unending joy—and the words of Jesus' promises lingered in the air around them:

"I will not leave you desolate; I will come to you."

"Peace I leave with you; my peace I give to you; not as the world gives do I give to you. Let not your hearts be troubled, neither let them be afraid."

That was all they had now—Jesus' promises—and they seemed so frail, so ephemeral, unable to bear the crushing weight of the reality of their lives.

So they gathered together—to mourn, to cry, to pray, perhaps to plan what their next moves would be. Would they trust Jesus' promises and step out on them to new life, or would they retreat, stepping back into a life immune to the promise of Jesus' words?

As the disciples gathered together, the text tells us, out of fear they shut the doors of the room in which they met. They closed the doors in order to shut the world out and themselves in. The world was too frightening, and they needed a safe place. They shut the doors "for fear of the Jews." For John the word "Jews" does not mean the Jewish people as a group, but rather stands for those religious authorities and powers that be who want things to stay the way they are, who resist the changes of new life. The disciples shut the doors for fear of the voices that told them Jesus was dead, that the world never would or could be different. The voices that threatened to extinguish all glimmers of hope in a new life. The disciples were afraid because those voices are so strong—the weight of the world resides with those voices—and the odds against the disciples' view of reality were tremendous. And so they gathered together in fear, seeking refuge and sanctuary.

We may want to ask, how could they, on Easter evening, on the very day of new life, how could they be so feeble, so timid, so afraid? Mary had seen the risen Lord—why were they afraid? They had heard Jesus' promises with their own ears—why did they seem so ready to accept defeat? How could they let their fears get the best of them?

How indeed? Dear brothers and sisters in Christ, as we gather together on this Pentecost day, we know that we, too, are afraid. We, too, have heard the words, "I have seen the Lord"; we, too, have listened to Jesus' promises. But there are days, oh so many days, when we are "sore afraid." Afraid of the decisions we have to make, the risks we have to take. Afraid of what happens if we do listen to Jesus' promises, afraid of what happens if we do not. Afraid because of our seeming helplessness in the face of situations of injustice that multiply daily. Afraid of being alone when even God's sustaining voice is hard to hear. Afraid simply of being. Afraid that the world is right—that death is the victor—and that we will live forever without hope and joy. Afraid that we will be crushed before we find the strength to be faithful to God's promises for our lives and our world.

We, like the disciples, are afraid, and so we, too, gather together in our room, our sanctuary, with the doors shut. Fear, of course, is not the only reason we seek sanctuary, but this room, this hour, provides a place of refuge for us. We gather here for Sunday morning worship and shut the doors because we know this is a safe place. It is all right to be afraid here. We come to this sanctuary because we can be afraid here. We can speak our fears honestly here in the gathering of those who cling desperately to Jesus' words of promise.

And so the disciples gather together, knowing that all they have to hold onto are Jesus' words for their future, for our future. It is the wonder of this Pentecost story that into this fearful, cloistered gathering, the risen Jesus came. The closed doors could not keep him out, and suddenly he stood among them and greeted them with these words, "Peace be with you." That was one of his promises, "My peace I give to you," and now it is fulfilled. And as he spoke to the disciples, he showed them his hands and his sides—and when they recognized him, their fear was changed to joy. This, too, had been his promise, "Do not be afraid"; "you have sorrow now, but I will see you again, and your hearts will rejoice, and no one will take your joy from you," and this promise too was fulfilled.

The disciples rejoiced in the sure knowledge that Jesus is a promise-maker and a promise-keeper. The faithfulness of Jesus, the faithfulness of God in Jesus, is the beginning point of new life for the church. The one who makes promises keeps them—and the reality shaped by this promise-keeper is to be trusted.

Jesus knew the disciples' needs and made himself completely available to them. He found them in their fearfulness and gave them joy and hope. He offered up his wounds to them; he spoke words of peace to them. And while the disciples rejoiced at Jesus' gift of peace, he kept one more promise—he breathed on them the breath of God and gave them the Holy Spirit. He created them anew for a new life, a life to be lived out beyond the closed doors.

The gift of the Holy Spirit was accompanied by a bold commission, "Receive the Holy Spirit. If you forgive the sins of any, they are forgiven them; if you retain the sins of any, they are retained." Jesus knew—and thus offers to his disciples—that the only hope for a new world rests in seeing ourselves and others differently. No sin is forgiven if we are determined to retain it. No matter how much penance is done, no life will ever be able to begin anew if we continue to keep score according to the old rules. We must let go of that which is past, forgive that which is past, in order to be available for the inbreaking of God's new world. In public politics, in personal relationships, in our families, in our treatment of ourselves, we must trust in the forgiving power of the Holy Spirit to work genuine transformation. We are not enslaved to the mistakes of our past—segregation, sex discrimination, inadequate public housing, failed human rights policies, a broken marriage, a breach with a child—because Jesus' gift of the Holy Spirit means that we can be transformed and begin anew.

But to be transformed we have to trust the promises of the one who comes among us. What we retain and count against one another and ourselves will never be transformed. We will never trust that we can move out of places, policies, and relations to which we feel doomed until we embrace the Spirit's promise of forgiveness. Through his words on forgiveness, Jesus exhorts his disciples to let the past be the past so that new life has a chance. The gift of the Holy Spirit marks a new beginning, new life, new creation.

The good news on this Pentecost Sunday, then, is this: into this sanctuary, with its doors shut, overflowing with our fears, the risen Jesus comes to breathe on us anew. Even when we shut the doors of the room, the house, our hearts; even when we shut the doors for fear, Jesus enters and transforms our fear to joy. Jesus is here—to offer us peace, to give us the Spirit of new life that makes it possible to open the doors and go forth into a new world, forgiven and forgiving.

This is the gift of Pentecost—the presence of the risen Jesus, assured by the Holy Spirit, that will come even here, even now, even among us, and give us peace. He is here, he is with us, and he has created us anew for life in the world.